NCC COMMON & SPECIAL SUBJECT SD/SW - ARMY

NCC B & C Certificate Exam

Subject Wise Multiple Choice Questions

1500 + MCQ

Dr. Ravinayak Patlavath

INDIA • SINGAPORE • MALAYSIA

ISBN 979-8-89610-676-0

Dedicated to

The Maharaja Sayajirao Gaekwad III

Contents

Special Subject (Army)

Preface

It is with great pleasure; we present this Multiple-Choice Questions (MCQ) book as a need of the hour for practising various topics of NCC. This book is designed for NCC cadets of Senior Division B and C certificate to achieve **A grade** in their NCC exams. Achieving A grade in NCC C- certificate will make cadets to be eligible to appear NCC special entry as well as Combined Defence Services Examination (CDS) interview. This book will help in improving the concepts of NCC topics for the cadets who are preparing for Youth exchange program and Best cadet. The book consists of topic wise many simple and complex multiple-choice questions, prepared based on the NCC syllabus published by DG NCC Govt. of India. The questions are carefully curated to challenge cadets understanding, encourage critical thinking, and promote active recall of information. Each topic is tailored to address key concepts. This book is divided into several chapters, each focusing on a specific subject or topic area. This format allows you to test your knowledge and immediately review your performance, facilitating an efficient learning process. Test your understanding and knowledge over the topics after thorough study of NCC books/Reference books published by DGNCC Govt. of India.

About the Author

Dr. Ravinayak Patlavath, Ex. ANO, served in NCC for 8 years at 3 Gujarat Battalion NCC Vadodara. He is currently holding the position of Assistant Professor at Department of Botany, Faculty of Science, The Maharaja Sayajirao University of Baroda. He completed NCC-C certificate with B grade from 25 Andhra Battalion NCC. He was appointed as direct commissioned ANO in the rank of Lieutenant by the Director general of NCC. He went for Direct commission training at OTA Kamptee in 2017. In training he was appointed as Senior Under officer and successfully secured A grade in both PRCN (4th position) and refresher course (6th position). He received Director General NCC Commendation card (2021), ADG Gujarat DTE appreciation and consolation prize for online video module at DTE level for his exceptional services to the NCC.

Dr. Ravinayak Patlavath, in his 8 years of NCC service (2016 to 2024), significantly contributed to the nation by promoting 21 cadets to join Indian Army and 32 cadets into RDC. His cadets received Defence Secretary Commendation, Governor's medal, ADG Appreciation and many more.

"Don't think that someone will come to help you to fulfil your dreams or achieve your goals. Believe in yourself and push yourself hard towards your goal." **Success comes when you have a vision and dedication.** Jai Hind.!

– Dr. Ravinayak Patlavath, Ex. ANO

Acknowledgments

Colonel (Retired). Surendra Pawan Kumar, SM.

COMMON SUBJECT
(Army/Navy/Air)

01

NCC General

1.1 AIMS, OBJECTIVES AND ORGANIZATION OF NCC

1. NCC came into existence through which one of the following parliament act?

   A. XXXI B. XXXI C. XXXI D. XXXI

2. NCC XXXI act passed in which year

   A. 15 July 1948 C. 15 July 1948
   B. 15 July 1948 D. 15 July 1948

3. Match the following about raising of NCC

Month and Year	NCC Wings
1. July 1952	A. NCC Army Senior Division (SD)- Boys
2. April 1950	B. NCC Army Senior Wing (SW)-Girls
3. July 1949	C. NCC Air wing
4. July 1948	D. NCC Naval wing

   A. 1D, 2C, 3B, 4A C. 1A, 2C, 3B, 4D
   B. 1A, 2B, 3C, 4D D. 1B, 2D, 3A, 4C

4. __________ wing of NCC was raised on 01 April 1950?

   A. Army Wing B. Air Wing
   B. Navy Wing D. Marine Wing

5. NCC is a ________

   A. Part of Army
   B. First line of defense
   C. Part of National Disaster Management Authority
   D. Second line of defense

6. What is the main objective of NCC?

   A. To promote sports activities
   B. To provide vocational training
   C. To train young boys and girls to be better citizens and future leaders
   D. To offer scholarships to students

7. What is the main aim of NCC in terms of character development?

   A. Academic excellence
   B. Physical fitness
   C. Financial success
   D. Potential leadership and responsible citizens

8. What is the purpose behind the creation of the University Corps?

   A. To aid in healthcare services
   B. To raise a second line of defense
   C. To promote cultural exchange
   D. To support diplomatic efforts

9. When did the present-day NCC formally come into existence?

   A. 15 July 1947
   B. 15 August 1947
   C. 15 August 1948
   D. 15 July 1948

10. NCC comes under __________

A. Defense ministry
B. Home ministry
B. Ministry of education
D. President of India

11. Who is the overall in charge of NCC?

A. Defense ministry
C. Home ministry
B. President
D. Director General NCC

12. The Motto of NCC is?

A. Unity and Integrity
B. Unity and self-less service
C. Duty, honor and leadership
D. Unity and Discipline

13. How many Aims are there in NCC?

A. 5
B. 6
C. 3
D. 4

14. The NCC Headquarters is situated/located in _______

A. Noida
C. Hyderabad
B. New Delhi
D. Shimla

15. Where are the "Officers Training Academies" (OTA) located?

A. Kamptee and Chennai
C. Gwalior and Pune
B. Kamptee and Gwalior
D. Pune and Delhi

16. The "Officers Training Academies" (OTA) located in which of the following Indian states?

A. Maharashtra and Madhya Pradesh
B. Rajasthan and Haryana
C. Karnataka and Gujarat
D. Kerala and Goa

17. The NCC Headquarters, headed by ________?

    A. Director General NCC
    B. COAS NCC
    C. Defense Minister of India
    D. President of India

18. The Director General of NCC holds an officer of the rank of ________

    A. Lieutenant General
    B. General
    C. Major General
    D. Field Marshal

19. How many NCC directorates are there in India?

    A. 19 B. 16 C. 17 D. 15

20. How many Group Headquarters are there in the country?

    A. 72 B. 88 C. 99 D. 102

21. What is the rank of an officer heading NCC directorate?

    A. Brigadier
    B. Colonel
    C. Lieutenant General
    D. Major General

22. Each NCC group Head quarter is headed by an officer of the rank of ________

    A. Brigadier
    B. Colonel
    C. Lieutenant General
    D. Major General

23. NCC group head quarter controls ________ NCC Battalions/units

    A. 3 to 5 B. 5 to 7 C. Up to 9 D. 4

24. Match the following: NCC and its directorates.

NCC	Number of NCC Directorates
I. Army wing	A. 3
II. Naval wing	B. 2
III. Air wing	C. 12

A. 1C, 2A, 3B
B. 1B, 2A, 3C
C. 1A, 2C, 3B
D. 1 C, 2B, 3A

25. Head of the NCC battalion is an officer of the rank of ___________

A. Brigadier
B. Lieutenant Colonel
C. Colonel
D. ANO

26. Each NCC battalion consists of companies (COY) which are commanded by ________.

A. Subedar Major
B. Lieutenant Colonel
C. Colonel
D. ANO

27. What is the role of Associate NCC Officers (ANOs)?

A. Commanding battalions
B. Providing training to cadets
C. Heading Group Headquarters
D. Managing civilian staff

28. OTA Kamptee is for ________ and Gwalior is for ___________

A. Men and Women
B. Both are for Women
C. Both are for Men
D. For Army soldiers

29. Who is an Associate NCC Officers (ANOs)?

    A. They are professors and teachers from colleges and schools
    B. They are doctors and Engineers
    C. They are regular army officers
    D. They are clerks of NCC

30. The regular officers in the NCC are drawn from______

    A. Army only
    B. Navy only
    C. Air force only
    D. All three services

31. Who are Girl Cadet Instructors (GCI) in the NCC?

    A. Female cadets appointed as leaders
    B. Officers responsible for conducting games to girls
    C. Instructors trained specifically to teach girls in the NCC
    D. Administrative staff overseeing recruitment procedures

32. Where do Permanent Instructional (PI) Staff come from?

    A. They are retired military personnel
    B. They are civilians with expertise in gliding and ship modeling
    C. They are regular officers serving in the NCC
    D. They are active-duty personnel from the Army, Navy, and Air Force

33. What role do Civilian Gliding Instructors and Ship Modelling Instructors play in the NCC?

A. They provide specialized training in aviation and maritime skills
B. They assist in administrative tasks within the NCC headquarters
C. They are responsible for organizing cultural events for cadets
D. They lead physical fitness sessions for cadets

34. What is the responsibility of Civilian Staff in the NCC?

A. Training cadets in marksmanship
B. Assisting with medical emergencies during training
C. Providing logistical support and administrative assistance
D. Conducting physical fitness assessments for cadets

35. Aims of NCC, choose the correct aims. / Which one of the following is an aim of NCC?

1. Character, Comradeship, Discipline, Secular Outlook, Spirit of Adventure, Ideals of selfless service
2. Creating a human resource of organized, trained and motivated youth
3. Providing an environment conducive to choose the Armed Forces as a career.

A. 1 and 2
C. 1, 2 and 3
B. 2 and 3
D. 1 and 3

36. Which one of the following is NOT an aim of NCC?

    A. To develop character
    B. To promote individualism
    C. To instill discipline
    D. To encourage a secular outlook

37. Regarding cadets' future careers NCC aims at________?

    A. To restrict their career choices
    B. To discourage them from joining the workforce
    C. To encourage them to pursue military careers
    D. To limit their leadership opportunities

38. Who wrote NCC Song?

    A. Shri Charanjit
    B. Fakaruddin Ali
    C. S. Bose
    D. Shri Ranjit Sinh

39. Match the following: NCC song and adopted year

NCC Song	Adopted Year
1. Kadam Mila Ke Chal	A. 1980
2. Hum Sab Hindi Hain	B. 1974
3. Hum Sab Bhartiya Hain	C. 1963

    A. 1C, 2A, 3B
    B. 1A, 2C, 3B
    C. 1B, 2A, 3C
    D. 1 C, 2B, 3A

1. A	2. A	3. A	4. B	5. D	6. C	7. D	8. B	9. D	10. A
11. A	12. D	13. C	14. B	15. B	16. B	17. A	18. A	19. C	20. C
21. D	22. A	23. B	24. D	25. C	26. D	27. B	28. A	29. A	30. D
31. C	32. D	33. A	34. C	35. C	36. B	37. C	38. A	39. D	

1.2 NCC CAMPS: TYPES AND CONDUCT

1. Regular parade is a ________ type of training

   A. Camp
   B. Institutional
   C. Army attachment
   D. Adventure

2. A regular NCC camp is of how many days ________

   A. 10 B. 12 C. 7 D. 9

3. Seamanship, Navigation, Communication are activities of ________

   A. Army wing
   B. Naval wing
   C. Airwing
   D. Paramilitary wing

4. Swimming, Scuba Diving and Wind Surfing are activities of ________

   A. Army wing
   B. Naval wing
   C. Airwing
   D. Paramilitary wing

5. Airmanship, Aero modelling, Navigation are activities of ________

   A. Army wing
   B. Naval wing
   C. Airwing
   D. Paramilitary wing

6. Air Frames, Aero Engines and Microlite Flying are activities of ________

   A. Army wing
   B. Naval wing
   C. Airwing
   D. Paramilitary wing

7. Which one of the following NCC wing has highest number of NCC directorates?

   A. Army B. Navy C. Air D. OTA

8. Which one of the following NCC wing has highest number of NCC group headquarters?

   A. Army B. Navy C. Air D. OTA

9. Which one of the following is/are activities conducted for NCC Naval wing cadets?

   A. Horse riding and veterinary care
   B. Airmanship and navigation
   C. Swimming and scuba diving
   D. Archery and fencing

10. Which of the following is NOT a part of the Naval Wing activities?

    A. Seamanship B. Aero modelling
    B. Navigation D. Communication

11. What are some of the activities conducted for the Air Wing cadets?

    A. Horse riding and veterinary
    B. Airmanship and microlite flying
    C. Swimming and scuba diving
    D. Archery and fencing

12. The primary focus of the Remount & Veterinary activity is?________

    A. Learning about aviation mechanics
    B. Seamanship and navigation
    C. Horsemanship and riding
    D. Military tactics and strategy

13. Which one of the following is NOT a part of NCC Air Wing activities?

A. Aero modelling
B. Navigation
C. Swimming
D. Airmanship

14. Which of the following is NOT a staffing component of the NCC?

A. Regular officers from the three services
B. Civilian Ship Modelling Instructors
C. Civilian Gliding Instructors
D. Local government officials

15. What type of training does the NCC emphasizes?

I. Administrative training
II. Camp training
III. Physical fitness training
IV. Institutional training

A. I and II
B. II, III and IV
C. I and IV
D. I, II, III and IV

16. Which type of training involves attachment with Army?

A. Institutional Training
B. Camp Training
C. Attachment Training
D. Field training

17. What is the primary aim of Camps in NCC?

A. To provide individual training to cadets
B. To impart collective training with emphasis on leadership development
C. To conduct academic lectures
D. To organize sports tournaments

18. How are camps planned?

    A. Without any consultation
    B. In consultation with educational institutions only
    C. In consultation with various agencies including educational institutions and district administration
    D. In consultation with the cadets and PI staff

19. Which type of camp aims to introduce cadets to a regimented way of life and emphasizes discipline and character building?

    A. Centrally Organised Camps
    B. Annual Training Camps
    C. Leadership Camps
    D. Thal Sainik Camp

20. What is the purpose of the Thal Sainik Camp?

    A. To provide exposure to Navy training
    B. To provide exposure to Army training and foster competitive spirit
    C. To provide exposure to Air Force training
    D. To provide exposure to leadership training

21. What is the duration of the Republic Day Camp (RDC)?

    A. 26 days
    B. 10 days
    C. 120 days
    D. 30 days

22. What is the primary objective of the Ek Bharat Shresth Bharat (EBSB) Camps?

    A. To foster international relations
    B. To promote cultural exchange and national integration

C. To provide military training
D. To conduct leadership workshops

23. What activities are conducted in the Ek Bharat Shresth Bharat Camps?

A. Only physical training
B. Cultural programs, quiz competitions, and demonstrations on national unity
C. Military drills
D. Sports tournaments

24. The acronym 'COC' stands for ________.

A. Cadet's Organization Camps
B. Centrally Organized Camps
C. Centralized Organizational Camps
D. Cadet Orientation Camps

25. What is the duration of the Centrally Organized Camps (COC)?

A. 5 days
B. 10 days
C. 12 days
D. 15 days

26. Which camp aims to expose selected SD/SW Cadets to the Armed Forces environment?

A. Thal Sainik Camp
B. Attachment Training IMA/OTA
C. Nau Sainik Camp
D. Rock Climbing Camp

27. What is the primary aim of the Rock-Climbing Camp?

    A. To expose cadets to the basics of elementary rock climbing and foster spirit of adventure and leadership qualities
    B. To imbibe environmental awareness and concern, inculcate respect for local customs.
    C. To give a feel of Military training which would give them confidence and inspire them to join the Armed Forces
    D. To provide exposure to naval and army training

28. What is the primary aim of Leadership Camps?

    A. To conduct physical training
    B. To develop leadership qualities in cadets and provide SSB training
    C. To organize cultural programs and SSB training
    D. To conduct firing fighting drills and leadership quality classes

29. Where is the Republic Day Camp (RDC) held annually?

    A. Mumbai
    B. Delhi
    C. Chennai
    D. Kolkata

30. Which camp is aimed at providing SSB training to the NCC cadets?

    A. Leadership Camps
    B. Army Attachment Camp
    C. Thal Sainik Camp
    D. SSB Screening Camp

31. What is the primary focus of the Annual Training Camps (ATCs)/Combined Annual Training Camps (CATCs)?

    A. To introduce cadets to a regimented way of life
    B. To provide academic studies and hostel life
    C. To foster physical fitness training and yoga
    D. To expose social media usage, singing and dancing

32. Who conducts the All-India Treks?

    A. State Governments under ADG
    B. District Administration under police supervision
    C. Designated State Directorates under aegis of DGNCC
    D. Ministry of youth affairs and sports

33. Spirit of adventure, leadership, stamina, endurance, self-confidence, team spirit as well as espirit-de-corps are the aims of ________ camp

    A. All India treks
    B. IMA
    C. Leadership camp
    D. RDC

34. What is the main objective of the Rock-Climbing Camps?

    A. To provide exposure to military training
    B. To develop leadership qualities
    C. To inculcate spirit of adventure and teamwork
    D. To organize sports competitions

35. Who conducts the Leadership Camps?

    A. IMA Dehradun
    B. Ministry of Defence
    C. Directorate General NCC
    D. State Governments

36. What is the aim of the All-India Treks conducted by DG NCC?

A. To provide exposure to military training
B. To enhance physical fitness
C. To develop leadership qualities
D. To imbibe environmental awareness and promote national integration

37. Match the following list

Camp Type	Organizer	Duration/ No. of days
1. ATC/CATC	a. HQ DG NCC	p. 10
2. RDC	b. Respective Units/ Battalions of under the Gp. Hq.	q. 12
3. Centrally Organized Camps (Thal Sainik/ All India Trek/Rock climbing/ Vayu Sainik/ Nau Sainik/ EBSB/ Leadership Camp/ Attachment camp)	c. IMA/OTA	r. 1st Jan to 29th Jan

A. 1ap, 2bq, 3cr
B. 1bp, 2ar, 3cq
C. 1bp, 2cr, 3aq
D. 1cr, 2aq, 3br

38. What is the duration of the Republic Day Camp (RDC)?

A. 1 week B. 2 weeks C. 3 weeks D. 4 weeks

39. How many EBSB camps are conducted every year?

    A. 10 B. 20 C. 30 D. 35

40. Every year in which camp Prime Minister's rally is held/conducted?

    A. Thal Sainik Camp
    B. Nau Sainik Camp
    C. Vayu Sainik Camp
    D. Republic Day Camp (RDC)

41. Among the following who inaugurates the NCC Republic Day camp?

    A. The Prime Minister of India
    B. The President of India
    C. The Vice President of India
    D. The Defence Minister of India

42. What activities are conducted during the Republic Day Camp (RDC)?

    A. Cultural Programmes
    B. Guard Of Honour
    C. Drill
    D. All of the above

43. What is the significance of the Prime Minister's Rally during the Republic Day Camp?

    A. To showcase the cultural diversity of India
    B. To award the Champion Directorate and Best Cadets
    C. To conduct survey of competitions
    D. To provide leadership training and motivation

44. Every year during Republic Day Camp Prime Minister's Rally will be held on____.

A. 28th January
B. 25th January
C. 26th January
D. 27th January

45. How are the Republic Day Camp (RDC) participants selected?

A. Through physical fitness
B. Based on academic performance
C. Based on their drill, proficiency, capabilities and skills in various competitions and events
D. By the recommendation of commanding officer

46. Match the following: Camp and place

Camp	Conducted at
1. Thal Sainik and RDC	P. Delhi
2. Nau Sainik	Q. Karwar
3. Vayu Sainik	R. Jodhpur

A. 1P, 2Q, 3R
B. 1Q, 2P, 3R
C. 1R, 2Q, 3P
D. 1P, 2R, 3Q

47. Identify the main objective and aim of the Ek Bharat Shresth Bharat (EBSB) Camps?

I. To promote international relations
II. To provide military training
III. To foster unity among different regions of India
IV. To organize cultural exchange programs

A. I and IV
B. II and III
C. III and IV
D. I and III

48. How are the participants selected for Ek Bharat Shresth Bharat (EBSB) Camps?

A. Based on physical fitness
B. Based on academic performance
C. Based on their skill and proficiency
D. By recommendation of their peers

49. What is the aim of the Ek Bharat Shresth Bharat (EBSB) Camps?

A. To promote international relations
B. To conduct scientific research
C. To organize adventure sports activities
D. To promote national integration among cadets

50. What is the main objective/aim of the Attachment Training IMA/OTA?

A. To provide leadership training
B. To conduct sports tournaments
C. To organize cultural programs
D. To provide exposure to officer training imparted at IMA/OTA

51. What is the primary purpose of the Military Attachment Camps?

A. To provide exposure to medical training
B. To familiarize cadets with the Armed Forces environment
C. To conduct social service activities
D. To organize quiz competitions

52. Which camp aims to expose selected SD/SW Cadets to the Armed Forces environment?

A. Attachment Training IMA/OTA
B. Thal Sainik Camp
C. Nau Sainik Camp
D. Rock Climbing Camp

53. Which camp aims to develop spirit of adventure, leadership qualities, and team spirit among cadets?

A. Thal Sainik Camp
B. Leadership Camps
C. Attachment Training IMA/OTA
D. Rock climbing Camps

54. What is the purpose of the SSB Screening Camps?

A. To provide exposure to military training
B. To conduct leadership training to join police forces
C. To prepare cadets for selection for induction into Armed Forces
D. To organize sports and participation in national games

55. Where are the SSB Screening Camps conducted?

I. Officers Training Academies
II. State Capitals
III. International Camps
IV. Centrally Organized Camps

A. I and IV
B. II and III
C. I and II
D. III and IV

56. What types of training activities are conducted during camps?

   A. Only physical training
   B. Only academic studies
   C. Various activities including PT/Yoga, drill, games, and cultural activities
   D. No specific training activities

57. What is camp routine in NCC?

   A. Only physical training sessions
   B. A structured routine including physical training, meals, rest periods, and cultural activities
   C. Unstructured routine with no specific activities
   D. Continuous academic studies

58. What is the significance of the All India Treks conducted by DG NCC?

   A. To promote self-confidence
   B. To enhance physical fitness and drill
   C. To develop leadership qualities to join forces
   D. To imbibe environmental awareness and promote national integration

59. What is the aim of the Annual Training Camps/ Combined Annual Training Camps (ATCs/CATCs)?

   A. To introduce cadets to hostel life and academic studies
   B. To promote physical fitness and yoga
   C. To introduce cadets to a regimented way of life and character building
   D. To provide cultural exchange programs

60. What is the duration of Annual Training Camps/ Combined Annual Training Camps (ATCs/ CATCs)?

A. 5 days
B. 7 days
C. 10 days
D.14 days

61. Centrally Organized Camps (COC) conducted for how many days?

A. 5 days
B. 7 days
C. 10 days
D. 12 days

62. What is the main focus of the PT/Yoga training during the camps?

A. To organize sports competitions
B. To promote cultural exchange
C. To develop leadership qualities
D. To enhance physical fitness

63. What is the purpose of the Washing/Bathing activity in the camp routine?

A. To spread diseases
B. To promote personal hygiene
C. To look bright and elegant
D. To promote physical fitness

64. Which camp aims to enhance the self-confidence of cadets and deepen their value systems?

A. Rock Climbing Camp
B. Attachment Training IMA/OTA
C. Leadership Camp
D. Republic Day Camp (RDC)

65. How do the All-India Treks contribute to the development of cadets?

    A. By promoting social evils and networking
    B. By enhancing physical fitness and leadership skills
    C. By organizing cultural exchange programs
    D. By conducting quiz and debate competitions in hills

66. Which camp aims to bridge the cultural gap among various states of India?

    A. Leadership Camp
    B. Republic Day Camp (RDC)
    C. Attachment Training IMA/OTA
    D. Ek Bharat Shresth Bharat Camp

67. What is the significance of the SSB Screening Camps?

    A. To promote personal hygiene
    B. To orient and prepare cadets for selection into Armed Forces
    C. To conduct cultural exchange programs
    D. To organize sports competitions

68. Which type of camp is aimed at bringing together cadets from various parts of the country to enable them to know the culture of different states?

    A. Leadership Camps
    B. Nau Sainik Camp
    C. Thal Sainik Camp
    D. Centrally Organised Camps (COC)

69. Which camp is the culmination of all NCC Training activities and is held at Cariappa/ Garrison Parade Grounds, Delhi Cantt?

A. Republic Day Camp (RDC)
B. Thal Sainik Camp
C. Nau Sainik Camp
D. Vayu Sainik Camp

70. What are the primary qualities emphasized during camp training in NCC?

A. Academic excellence
B. Physical fitness `
C. Discipline, character, confidence building, and first aid
D. Social networking

1. B	2. A	3. B	4. B	5. C	6. C	7. A	8. A	9. C	10. B
11. B	12. C	13. C	14. D	15. B	16. C	17. B	18. C	19. B	20. B
21. D	22. B	23. B	24. B	25. C	26. B	27. A	28. B	29. B	30. A
31. A	32. C	33. A	34. C	35. C	36. D	37. B	38. D	39. D	40. D
41. C	42. D	43. B	44. A	45. C	46. A	47. C	48. C	49. D	50. D
51. B	52. A	53. D	54. C	55. A	56. C	57. B	58. D	59. C	60. C
61. D	62. D	63. B	64. D	65. B	66. D	67. B	68. D	69.A	70. C

1.3 INCENTIVES TO CADETS

1. What is the benefit for NCC 'C' Certificate holders in terms of recruitment for officers in the Army, Navy, and Air Force?

A. They are exempt from medical tests
B. They receive direct appointments without interviews

C. They are allotted specific vacancies in the respective services
D. They receive scholarships for further education

2. How are NCC cadets selected as officers in the Army after obtaining the 'C' Certificate?

A. Through UPSC written exams
B. Via direct appointment without any selection process
C. By clearing the SSB interview and medical test
D. By obtaining recommendation letters from NCC officers

3. How many seats per year at OTA are reserved for male candidates holding the NCC 'C' Certificate?

A. 76 B. 100 C. 120 D. 150

4. What percentage of vacancies are reserved for Girl candidates holding NCC 'C' certificate in OTA?

A. 5% B. 7% C. 10% D. 12%

5. In the Navy, how many seats per course are reserved for NCC 'C' certificate holders?

A. 3 B. 4 C. 5 D. 6

6. What percentage of vacancies are reserved for NCC 'C' certificate holders in the all courses of Air Force?

A. 5% B. 7% C. 10% D. 12%

7. In Air Force Academy how many seats are reserved for Girl candidates holding NCC 'C' certificate.

A. 2% B. 3% C. 5% D. 7%

8. UPSC conducts ________ exam for recruiting officers into Army, Navy and Air force.

   A. CDSE   B. CSE   C. SSB   D. DSE

9. Who are exempted from written exam of UPSC CDSE exam?

   A. All grades of NCC C certificates
   B. All grades of NCC A certificates
   C. All grades of NCC B certificates
   D. A and B grade of NCC C certificate

10. Other than defense sector NCC 'C' certificate holders receive bonus marks for job recruitment in_______.

   A. Corporate sector only
   B. State Govt. Services and private sectors
   C. Anganwadi and healthcare sector
   D. Educational institutions

11. Match the following

SL. No	Various Defence training Academies	Location/City	State
1.	India Military Academy (IMA)	A. Ezhimala	P. Telangana
2.	India Naval Academy (INA)	B. Hyderabad	Q. Tamil Nadu
3.	India Airforce Academy (IAA)	C. Chennai	R. Uttarakhand
4.	Officers Training Academy	D. Dehradun	S. Kerala

A. 1DR, 2AS, 3BP, 4CQ
B. 1AS, 2DR, 3CQ, 4BP
C. 1DP, 2BQ, 3AR, 4CS
D. 1CR, 2 BP, 3AS, 4DQ

12. Identify the correct statements.

Assertion: The NCC is a voluntary organization which is administered through the Ministry of Defence. provide opportunities various public and private sectors for NCC C certificate holders.

Reason: Girl cadets of NCC C certificate holders can get employment within NCC as Whole Time Lady Officer, Girl Cadet Instructor, Aero and Ship Modelling Instructor.

A. Both Assertion (A) and Reason (R) are the true and Reason (R) is a correct explanation of Assertion (A)
B. Both Assertion (A) and Reason (R) are the true but Reason (R) is not a correct explanation of Assertion (A)
C. Assertion (A) is true and Reason (R) is false
D. Assertion (A) is false and Reason (R) is true

13. NCC 'B'/'C' certificate holders are given preference by state governments for recruitment in which department?

A. Education Department
B. Agriculture Department
C. Police Service
D. Tourism Department

14. Which one of the following departments offers preference to NCC 'B'/'C' certificate holders for recruitment in various states?

1. Health Department	2. Transport Department	3. Finance Department
4. Housing Department	5. Energy Department	6. Forest Department
7. Excise Department	8. Commerce Department	9. Science and Technology
10. Customs Department	11. Labor Department	12. Immigration Department

A. 2, 6 and 7
B. 8, 3 and 9
C. 5, 1 and 4
D. 10, 11 and 12

15. NCC Girl Cadets preferred for in various state government departments for the jobs of________.

A. Engineers and technicians
B. Nurses, receptionists, and telephone operators
C. Police officers
D. Lawyers and legal advisors

16. Cadet's Welfare Society (CWS) annually awards scholarship of Rs.________ per cadet for 1000 NCC cadets to academically brilliant students.

A. Rs 1000 B. Rs 3000 C. Rs 4500 D. Rs 6000

17. Every year how many NCC cadets receive the scholarship from CWS?

A. 500 B. 750 C. 1000 D. 1500

18. What is the amount of prize money given to the "Best Cadet Award" granted at Group level by CWS is?

A. Rs 1500 B. Rs 2500 C. Rs 3500 D. Rs 4500

19. How much is the prize money granted for the "2nd Best Cadet Award" at Group level by CWS?

A. Rs 1500 B. Rs 2500 C. Rs 3500 D. Rs 4500

20. In which of the following fields NCC C certificate holders get special quotas in admission?
    1. Vocational training programs.
    2. Art and music courses
    3. Degree and diploma courses
    4. Sports coaching programs
    5. Legal studies (LLB) courses
    6. Hospitality management courses
    7. Journalism and mass communication programs
    8. Dance academies
    9. Culinary institutes
    10. Government polytechnics and engineering colleges
    11. Medical courses
    12. Fashion design programs
    13. Interior design courses

A. 1, 4, 6 and 8 C. 9, 12 and 13
B. 3, 5, 10 and 11 D. 2, 7 and 5

1. C	2. C	3. B	4. C	5. D	6. C	7. C	8. A	9. D	10. B
11. A	12. A	13. C	14. A	15. B	16. D	17. C	18. D	19. C	20. B

1.4 DUTIES OF NCC CADETS

1. In National Cadet Core (NCC), the term "Cadet" stands for ________.

   A. Trainer B. Trainee C. Officer D. Soldier

2. Qualifications for enrolment in the Senior Division/ Senior Wing of NCC is ________.
   1. Citizen of India or Nepal
   2. Citizen of any country and having criminal records
   3. Must be on the roll of the College which is providing the unit or part thereof
   4. Must satisfy physical fitness standard specified
   5. Must be member of Any communal organization or political organization

   A. All are correct
   B. 2, 4 and 5 are correct
   C. 1, 3 and 4 are correct
   D. 3, 4 and 5 are correct

3. What are some advantages of being an NCC cadet?
   1. Access to free healthcare services
   2. Priority for some government jobs
   3. Chance to take part in disaster relief tasks
   4. Opportunity to visit foreign countries

   A. All are correct
   B. 2 and 3 are correct
   C. 2, 3 and 4 are correct
   D. 1 and 4 are correct

4. Which of the following is NOT an advantage of being an NCC cadet?

   A. Chance to take part in disaster relief tasks
   B. Opportunity to attend NCC camps like ATC, CATC, NIC, COC and YEP.
   C. Preference for joining armed forces and other forces
   D. Guaranteed employment in the private sector

5. What is one of the most basic traits expected from an NCC cadet?

   A. Laziness
   B. Indiscipline
   C. Self-discipline
   D. Obeying orders

   A. C and D
   B. A and B
   C. B and C
   D. A and D

6. What is one of the duties of an NCC cadet during parades and camps?

   A. Arriving late
   B. Disobeying orders
   C. Participating with complete enthusiasm
   D. Ignoring cultural activities

7. Which of the following is NOT a duty/responsibility of the NCC cadet with respect to cadets personal grooming and uniform?

   A. Taking proper haircuts
   B. Wearing clean and correct pattern of uniform
   C. Pressing uniforms irregularly
   D. Wearing beret in the correct manner

8. Which one of the following is a responsibility of an NCC cadet regarding?

   A. Avoiding team work
   B. Ignoring cultural activities
   C. Pursuing adventure activities
   D. Not attending parades regularly

9. Assertion: social awareness initiatives, environmental issues, disaster relief, adventure and sports activities and other nation building efforts are part of NCC training/life.
   Reason: The main aims of NCC i.e., becoming a potential leader with character qualities and responsible citizen in all walks of life espousing the noble values and objectives of NCC.

   A. Both Assertion (A) and Reason (R) are the true and Reason (R) is a correct explanation of Assertion (A).
   B. Both Assertion (A) and Reason (R) are the true but Reason (R) is not a correct explanation of Assertion (A).
   C. Assertion (A) is true and Reason (R) is false.
   D. Assertion (A) is false and Reason (R) is true.

10. Obeying the orders of higher ranks is a ________

    A. Aim of NCC
    B. Social responsibility
    C. Objective of NCC
    D. Duty of NCC cadet

11. How NCC cadets are expected to contribute in nation-building?

    A. Through academic achievements
    B. By ignoring social issues

C. Through active participation in social, environmental, and disaster relief initiatives
D. By avoiding leadership roles

12. How NCC cadets are expected to extend beyond their training after passing out from NCC?

A. They are expected to focus solely on their NCC duties
B. They are expected to forget their NCC training once they leave the institution
C. They are expected to carry forward their responsibilities to all fields they engage in the future
D. They are expected to focus on personal goals only

13. 'Cadets Commandments' are given by ________.

A. Director General NCC
B. President of India
C. Home minister of India
D. Prime minister of India

14. Which of the following is NOT a part of 'Cadets Commandments' given by the Director General, NCC?

A. Ensuring construction of toilets
B. Avoiding helping accident victims
C. Promoting digital transactions
D. Donating blood annually

15. 'Cadets Commandments', a cadet must plant minimum ________ trees in a year.

A. One B. Two C. Three D. Four

16. As per the 'Cadets Commandments' by what age NCC cadets must obtain voter and PAN cards?

    A. Obtaining them after the age of 21
    B. Obtaining them after the age of 18
    C. Not obtaining them at all
    D. Obtaining them only if necessary

17. Regarding social service, which of the following is NOT a part of the 'Cadets Commandments'.

    A. Donating blood
    B. Undertaking 100 hours of shramdaan
    C. Helping physically-challenged persons
    D. Avoiding garbage segregation

18. According to the 'Cadets Commandments', A cadet should uphold ________ even when not under observation.

    A. Secular outlook
    B. Unity
    C. Regional bias
    D. Discipline

19. With respect to 'Cadets Commandments' a NCC cadet must take part in ________many hours of shramdaan

    A. 20
    B. 100
    C. 70
    D. 80

1. B	2. C	3. C	4. D	5. A	6. C	7. C	8. C	9. A	10. D
11. C	12. C	13. A	14. B	15. B	16. B	17. D	18. D	19. B	

02

National Integration and Awareness

2.1 NATIONAL INTEGRATION: IMPORTANCE AND NECESSITY

1. What is national integration?

   A. Economic development
   B. Political stability
   C. Military cooperation
   D. Feeling of togetherness and unity among the people

2. Which of the following is NOT a part of national integration?

   A. Social integration
   B. Cultural integration
   C. Economic integration
   D. Technological integration

3. Why national integration is important?

   A. To maintain cultural diversity
   B. To ensure survival and prosperity of a nation
   C. To promote competition among regions
   D. To focus on individual growth

4. Which of the following organization in India is actively involved in promoting national integration?

   A. Indian Army
   B. Sports Authority of India
   C. NCC (National Cadet Corps)
   D. Indian Space Research Organization

5. What do you mean by cultural integration?

   A. Losing one's cultural identity
   B. Complete assimilation into another culture
   C. Exchange of beliefs and rituals while maintaining one's own culture
   D. Rejecting foreign cultural practices

6. Which of the following is a reason for economic inequality in India?

   A. Inflation
   B. Cultural diversity
   C. Language barriers
   D. Political stability

7. One of the main causes of unemployment in India is_______.?

   A. Overpopulation
   B. Lack of skills
   C. Underemployment of people
   D. Over-education

8. What has led to an increase in inequality in rural areas of India?

   A. The Green Revolution
   B. Urban migration
   C. Economic reforms
   D. Industrialization

9. Identify the way to achieve political integration?

   A. By involving religion in politics
   B. By enforcing laws against political exploitation
   C. By focusing on caste-based politics
   D. By creating regional parties

10. Religious integration requires ________.3

    A. Uniform religious practices
    B. A single national religion
    C. Tolerance and respect for other religions
    D. Banning religious practices

11. What kind of identity is important for national integration?

    A. Regional identity
    B. Common national identity
    C. Cultural identity
    D. Religious identity

12. Which aspect of social integration is important for minority groups?

    A. Learning a common language and adopting common values
    B. Separation from mainstream society
    C. Maintaining their cultural isolation
    D. Creating separate communities

13. What is necessary for maintaining peace and harmony in a nation?

    A. Mutual distrust
    B. Feeling of togetherness among the people
    C. Military force
    D. Segregation of communities

14. How does national integration contribute to the development of a nation?

    A. It helps the nation to grow and develop
    B. It encourages competition between regions
    C. It creates divisions among communities
    D. It hinders economic progress

15. What is one way to ensure law and order in a country?

    A. By giving preference to specific communities
    B. By allowing regional laws to take precedence
    C. By limiting the rights of minority groups
    D. By ensuring equal rights and opportunities for all

16. What is the role of national festivals in promoting national integration?

    A. They highlight regional differences
    B. They celebrate individual achievements
    C. They act as a unifying force for the country
    D. They focus on local traditions only

17. Which of the following is a characteristic of social integration?

    A. Isolation of minority groups
    B. Respect for common laws and values
    C. Maintenance of cultural divisions
    D. Promotion of regional languages

18. Which of the following is necessary for the welfare and well-being of the people in a nation?

    A. Mutual understanding and cooperation
    B. Focus on individual development

C. Increased competition among communities
D. Isolation of different cultural groups

19. Why national integration is important in a country like India?

A. Because of its small population
B. Because of its economic prosperity
C. Because of its diversity in language, religion, and culture
D. Because of its political unity

20. What is the relationship between national integration and nation-building?

A. They are opposing concepts
B. National integration hinders nation-building
C. National integration and nation-building are synonymous
D. Nation-building is more important than integration

1. D	2. D	3. B	4. C	5. C	6. A	7. C	8. A	9. B	10. C
11. B	12. A	13. B	14. A	15. D	16. C	17. B	18. A	19. C	20. C

2.2 FACTORS AFFECTING NATIONAL INTEGRATION

1. One of the main factors affecting national integration in India is _______.

A. Economic equality
B. Technological advancement
C. Casteism
D. Globalization

2. What is India's cultural composition?

    A. Homogeneous
    B. Multi-racial and multi-religious
    C. Monolingual
    D. Unilateral

3. What is the role of political manipulation play in national integration?

    A. It promotes unity
    B. It encourages economic growth
    C. It leads to disintegration and communal riots
    D. It helps resolve religious differences

4. Which of the following is a consequence of illiteracy?

    A. Increased employment
    B. Easy exploitation by vested interests
    C. Improved political stability
    D. Decreased regionalism

5. Casteism created ________ in Indian society.

    A. Equality among all communities
    B. Economic prosperity for all castes
    C. Unity in diversity
    D. A wide gulf between different segments of society

6. Which factor has contributed to linguistic tensions in India?

    A. National unity
    B. Economic equality
    C. Multi-linguism
    D. Political stability

7. The unequal development of different regions will lead to________.

   A. National prosperity
   B. Divisive tendencies and conflicts
   C. Increased social harmony
   D. A decline in regional pride

8. How many officially recognized languages are there in India?

   A. 10 B. 12 C. 15 D. 20

9. What is social disparity?

   A. Inequality in society based on unequal distribution of goods, services, and wealth
   B. Equal distribution of wealth
   C. Regional competition
   D. Political stability

10. What is one of the major causes of ethnic conflicts in India?

    A. Ethnic nationalism
    B. Economic equality
    C. Caste equality
    D. Unemployment

11. What does tribal identity represent?

    A. Inferiority and primitivity
    B. Pride in self-understanding
    C. Cultural superiority
    D. Assimilation into mainstream society

12. What has corruption and lack of character caused in the country?

    A. Economic prosperity
    B. Political stability
    C. Moral upliftment
    D. Immense damage to the nation

13. What does the "Philosophy of Integration" emphasize for national integration?

    A. Nationalism and patriotism alone
    B. Continuous and vigorous efforts by every citizen
    C. Separation of regional identities
    D. Individual gain

14. What is the role of education in national integration?

    A. To promote regionalism
    B. To emphasize caste and religion
    C. To motivate future citizens of the nation
    D. To segregate different communities

15. What is essential for achieving emotional unity among the people?

    A. Political control
    B. People considering themselves as one
    C. Regional divisions
    D. Economic independence

16. How can media be used effectively for national integration?

    A. By introducing people to different cultures and stressing common elements
    B. By promoting regional differences

C. By spreading political ideologies
D. By avoiding discussions on national unity

17. What should be done to promote secularism in a multi-religious society?

A. Encourage religious favoritism
B. Prohibit activities that create communal reactions
C. Promote communal reactions
D. Limit religious freedom

18. How can economic unity contribute to national integration?

A. By allowing economic disparity to continue
B. By focusing only on regional economic growth
C. By eliminating central government support
D. By providing special assistance to backward classes and minority groups

19. What is a key message to teach children for achieving national integration?

A. Focus on individual identity
B. We are all Indians belonging to one Motherland
C. Emphasize regional differences
D. Focus on technology

1. C	2. B	3. C	4. B	5. D	6. C	7. B	8. C	9. A	10. A
11. B	12. D	13. B	14. C	15. B	16. A	17. B	18. D	19. B	

2.3 UNITY IN DIVERSITY

1. Which statement best describes "unity in diversity" in India?

   A. India has a uniform religion
   B. India has one language and culture
   C. People of different backgrounds live harmoniously
   D. India does not value diversity

2. India's geographical unity extended from ________ to ________

   A. Rajasthan to Gujarat
   B. Punjab to assam
   C. Kashmir to kanyakumari
   D. Odisha to tamil nadu

3. The significant binding factor in India's national unity is________.

   A. Food habits
   B. Traditions
   C. Festivals
   D. The constitution

4. In India, which religion promotes dharma and karma?

   A. Buddhism
   B. Hinduism
   C. Sikhism
   D. Islam

5. What does Indian philosophy emphasize as the ultimate aim?

   A. Wealth
   B. Materialism
   C. Salvation
   D. Political power

6. Which of the following is a symbol of India's cultural unity?

   A. Individual festivals
   B. National anthem
   C. Dress code
   D. Kumbh mela

7. What is a common practice in Indian society towards others?

   A. Ignoring others
   B. Following a single custom
   C. Offering alms
   D. Focusing on material wealth

8. Which article of the constitution highlights India as a union of states?

   A. Article 1
   B. Article 14
   C. Article 21
   D. Article 44

9. Which leader first unified India under one umbrella?

   A. Ashoka
   B. Akbar
   C. Chandragupta Maurya
   D. Harsha

10. What role does Sanskrit play in India's emotional unity?

    A. It is spoken widely
    B. It brings different languages together
    C. It is the official language
    D. It is the language of majority

11. The motto of NCC is?

    A. Unity in diversity
    B. Discipline and power
    C. Unity and discipline
    D. Nation first

12. The primary role of NCC is?

    A. Spreading religion
    B. Nation-building and character-building
    C. Promoting material wealth
    D. Focusing only on academics

13. Which is not an activity under NCC's social service initiatives?

    A. Tree plantation
    B. Awareness rallies
    C. Blood donation camps
    D. Promoting caste system

14. One-way NCC cadets can contribute to adult education by?

    A. Helping with national education
    B. Training in sports only
    C. Ignoring illiteracy
    D. Organizing fashion shows

15. Which activity do NCC cadets engage in to protect the environment?

    A. Water wasting
    B. Petroleum exploration
    C. Plastic production
    D. Tree plantation drives

16. NCC promotes which language as part of its national duty?

    A. English   B. Sanskrit   C. Tamil   D. Hindi

17. NCC cadets pledge to treat all individuals as:

    A. Competitors   C. Subordinates
    B. Equals   D. Unimportant

18. An NCC initiative aimed at reducing gender discrimination is:

    A. Female foeticide pledge   C. Caste promotion
    B. Political campaign   D. Tree plantation

19. NCC's blood donation drives primarily help those who are:

    A. In financial need
    B. In the defense forces
    C. In urgent need of blood
    D. Well-off

20. The ultimate goal of NCC training is to:

    A. Create a powerful military force
    B. Develop responsible and disciplined citizens
    C. Build wealthy individuals
    D. Focus on sports only

1. C	2. C	3. D	4. B	5. C	6. D	7. D	8. A	9. C	10. B
11. C	12. B	13. D	14. A	15. D	16. D	17. B	18. A	19. C	20. B

2.4 THREATS TO NATIONAL SECURITY

1. What does national security aim to protect within a country?

   A. Only economic growth
   B. Security within borders
   C. International relations
   D. Religious freedom

2. Which ministry handles internal security in India?

   A. Ministry of external affairs
   B. Ministry of defense
   C. Ministry of home affairs
   D. Ministry of finance

3. What is a primary cause of internal threats in India?

   A. Poverty
   B. Religious homogeneity
   C. Export policies
   D. Immigration restrictions

4. Which country's border dispute has been a longstanding external threat for India?

   A. Bangladesh
   B. China
   C. Sri Lanka
   D. Myanmar

5. Which term describes terrorism supported by Pakistan-based groups in J&K?

   A. Islamist terrorism
   B. Domestic terrorism
   C. Cross-border terrorism
   D. Cyber terrorism

6. Which country is noted for being a base for insurgent groups like ULFA?

   A. Nepal
   B. Bhutan
   C. Myanmar
   D. Bangladesh

7. What type of threat does the China Pakistan relationship pose to India?

   A. Cultural
   B. Political
   C. Nuclear
   D. Economic

8. One key attribute of national security is ________.

   A. Securing economic resources
   B. Ensuring religious dominance
   C. Protecting territorial integrity
   D. Promoting international trade

9. What is a primary factor in India's national security doctrine?

   A. Political stability
   B. Religious supremacy
   C. Economic dominance
   D. Control over media

10. Which socio-economic issue is often a root cause of internal threats?

    A. Agricultural production
    B. Urban development
    C. Export losses
    D. Unemployment

11. What is a recommended approach for addressing regional aspirations?

    A. Military force
    B. Soft and sympathetic approach
    C. Strict laws only
    D. Complete negotiation

12. Poor governance is often exploited by________.

    A. International partners
    B. Government employees
    C. Criminals
    D. Tech industry

13. Which act's removal has been demanded due to perceived police atrocities?

    A. Arms act
    B. National security act
    C. AFSPA
    D. POTA

14. Intelligence in national security involves both:

    A. Defensive and offensive strategies
    B. Domestic and foreign tourism
    C. Internal and external trade
    D. Cultural and religious harmony

15. How long is India's land border with other countries?

    A. 8,000 km
    B. 10,000 km
    C. 15,000 km
    D. 20,000 km

16. Which area is emphasized as requiring coordinated border security efforts?

    A. Air borders
    B. Coastal security
    C. Land borders only
    D. Railway security

17. Cybersecurity became a highlighted issue after revelations by:

    A. Julian Assange
    B. NSA officials
    C. Wikileaks team
    D. Edward snowden

18. India's internal security doctrine emphasizes:

    A. Equitable growth
    B. Maintaining ethnic supremacy
    C. Frequent media censorship
    D. Promoting a single religion

19. Which organization in India is responsible for coordinating multi-agency intelligence efforts?

    A. CBI B. MAC C. NSA D. RAW

1. B	2. C	3. A	4. B	5. C	6. D	7. C	8. C	9. A	10. D
11. B	12. C	13. C	14. A	15. C	16. B	17. D	18. A	19. B	

03

Drill

1. Who introduced/invented/Initiated drill?

   A. Major Gen. Drall
   B. Major Gen. Drill
   C. Gen. Fedel Castro
   D. German Gen. Hitler

2. In which year drill came to existence

   A. 1490 B. 1666 C. 1857 D. 1947

3. Why drill is required/purpose of drill is?

   A. To control civilians
   B. To control animals
   C. To control soldiers
   D. To control students

4. What was the purpose of initiating drill in the army?

   A. To instill discipline, turnout, and team spirit
   B. To prepare for battles
   C. To entertain soldiers
   D. To increase the military budget

5. What is the significance of drill in military operations?

   A. It has little effect on military discipline.
   B. It has proved beneficial in maintaining discipline in previous battles.
   C. It is only useful for physical exercise.
   D. It is outdated and not relevant anymore.

6. “Team spirit” refers to ________

   A. Collaboration and unity among soldiers
   B. Competitive nature of soldiers
   C. Personal aspirations of soldiers
   D. Individual skills of soldiers

7. Who was Major General Dral?

   A. A German philosopher
   B. A military strategist
   C. A leader of the army
   D. A historian

8. What is the definition of Drill?

   A. A military operation
   B. A ceremonial event
   C. Conducting a procedure in a sequential and appropriate manner
   D. A form of physical exercise

9. How many types of Drill are there?

   A. 1 B. 2 C. 3 D. 4

10. What is the difference between Open Drill and Close Drill?

    A. Open Drill is conducted indoors, while Close Drill is conducted outdoors.
    B. Open Drill is conducted in field, while Close Drill is conducted in a parade ground.
    C. Open Drill is conducted in a field, while Close Drill is conducted indoors.
    D. Open Drill is conducted without any specific location, while Close Drill is conducted in a designated area.

11. ________ is the foundation of drill

A. Discipline
B. Turnout
C. Loud voice
D. DMS Shoes

12. ________ can be determined by observing Drill?

A. The proficiency of soldiers in combat
B. The level of physical fitness of soldiers
C. The discipline and morale of a unit
D. The effectiveness of military tactics

13. What are the purposes of Drill?

I. Discipline is the foundation of Drill.
II. Developing the habit of working together and obeying orders.
III. Assessing cadet's physical wellness.
IV. Training officers, JCOs, and NCOs command and control.
V. Teaching how to wear a uniform and walk.

A. I, III and V
B. I, II, IV and V
C. II, III, IV and V
D. II, III and IV

14. What are the three principles of Drill?

I. Smartness (furti).
II. Steadiness (sthirta).
III. Coordination (milkar kaam karna).
IV. Creative(rachnatmak)

A. I, III and III
B. I, II and IV
C. II, III and IV
D. III and IV

15. What is the technique described in "Foot Drill Ke Usul"?

    A. Shoot the left foot backward (paon ko tejii se piche nikalna)
    B. Shoot the right foot upward (paon ko teji se upper pehkna)
    C. Shoot the left foot forward. (paon ko teji se aage nikalna)
    D. Shoot the right foot downward (paon ko teji se niche pehkna)

16. Which of the following is listed as a bad habit in Drill?

    A. Rolling of eyes.
    B. Clicking the heel
    C. Dragging of foot.
    D. All of the above

17. Which factor determines the correctness of a word of command?

    I. Loudness (Swar)
    II. Clarity (Safai)
    III. Pitch
    IV. Timing
    V. Slowness

    A. All
    B. I, II, III and IV
    C. None
    D. only IV and V

18. Why loudness is important in delivering a word of command?

    A. To create confusion
    B. To maintain secrecy
    C. To ensure everyone hears it clearly
    D. To intimidate the squad

19. A correct word of command depends on the ________ of the voice and the correct word of command is given in a ________ so that it can be immediately followed to execute the command.

    A. "tone and pitch"; "clear and loudness of voice"
    B. "Articulation"; "pronunciation of voice"
    C. "Volume"; "speed of voice"
    D. "High tone and high pitch"; "slow and clear voice"

20. What is the importance of timing in giving a word of command?

    A. It creates suspense and slows the response
    B. It ensures immediate action to be taken
    C. It confuses the squad and make them frighten
    D. It delays the response and allows for discussion

21. Which of the following aspect emphasizes the coordination of the tongue, lips, and teeth while delivering the word of command?

    A. Loudness (Swar)
    B. Clarity (Safai)
    C. Pitch
    D. Timing

22. A word of command consists of how many parts?

    A. 1
    B. 2
    C. 3
    D. 4

23. A word of command is always given in ________ position.

    A. Vishram/At ease
    B. Savdhan/Attention
    C. Sitting down
    D. Lying down

24. Always to execute the word of command squad will be in ________ position. Or In which ever the position squad will come to ________ position and execute the word of command

A. Vishram/At ease
B. Sitting down
C. Savdhan/Attention
D. Lying down

25. The word of command "Savdhan" always used for________ .

I. To engaging in casual conversation
II. To beginning any drill movement
III. When sitting down
IV. When receiving an order or communicating with a senior

A. I and II
B. II and IV
C. III and IV
D. II and III

26. What is the correct posture described for the word of command "Savdhan"?

I. Both feet joined and toes at a 30-degree angle.
II. Both knees bent.
III. Both arms free at the sides with fists open naturally.
IV. Pants pulled up, chest lifted, shoulders pulled back, neck aligned with the collar, chin up, and eyes forward.

A. I and IV
B. II and III
C. III and IV
D. II and IV

27. The word of command "Vishram" is used for ________.

    I. After completing a conversation with a senior
    II. At the beginning of a drill movement
    III. After completing a drill movement
    IV. During a drill movement

    A. I and IV
    B. I and III
    C. II and IV
    D. II and III

28. What is the correct posture described for the word of command "Vishram"?

    I. Both knees bent.
    II. Both arms behind, left hand down and right hand up, fingers pointing downwards, right thumb over the left thumb.
    III. Weight of the body on both feet.
    IV. Both feet apart by 12 inches.
    V. Both arms free at the sides with fists open naturally.
    VI. Upon the command "Aram se," loosen the upper part of the body but keep the feet still.

    A. All are correct
    B. I, III and V
    C. II, III, IV and V
    D. II, III, IV and VI

29. In "Savdhan distance between toes is ________

    A. 6inch B. 12 Inch C. 18 Inch D. 8Inch

30. In "Savdhan angle between heels is________

    A. 30° B. 45° C. 0° D. 90°

31. In "Vishram" distance between toes is ________

    A. 6 Inch B. 12 Inch C. 18 Inch D. 8 Inch

32. In Vishram distance between heels is ________

    A. 6 Inch B. 12 Inch C. 18 Inch D. 8 Inch

33. Match the following

Khade Khade Mudna/ Turning while standing	Degrees of rotation/ Turning from "Savdhan"
P. Right Turn/ Dahine Mudna	1. 90° left
Q. Left Turn/ Baen Mudna	2. 45° to the right or left
R. About Turn/ Pichhe Mudna	3. 90° right
S. Half right or half left/ Aadha Dahine Aur Baen Mudna	4. 180°

A. P1, Q2, R3, S4
B. P2, Q3, R4, S1
C. P4, Q3, R2, S1
D. P3, Q1, R4, S2

34. How is "Half right or Half left/ Aadha Dahine Aur Baen Mudna" different from "Right turn /Dahine Mudna and Left turn /Baen mudna"?

    A. In "Half Right and Left Turn," we turn 90 degrees to the right or left
    B. In "Half Right and Left Turn," we turn 45 degrees to the right or left
    C. In "Half Right and Left Turn," we turn 180 degrees to the right or left
    D. In "Half Right and Left Turn," we turn 360 degrees to the right or left

35. Word of command "Savdhan, Vishram, Dahine Mudna, Baen Mudna, Piche Mudna or Adha Dahine ya Baen Mudna the leg should rise to a height of ________ to execute the command.

A. 8 Inch B. 10 Inch C. 12 Inch D. 6 Inch

36. Why is precise sizing/Kadwar Sizing is always necessary in drills?

A. To ensure everyone stands in a straight line
B. To make sure the tallest person stands at the far right and the shortest at the far left
C. To maintain uniformity and aesthetics, especially when viewed from a distance
D. To facilitate easy conduction of drill exercises

37. When precise sizing/Kadwar Sizing is always necessary in drills?

A. Ceremonial Drill C. Guard mounting
B. Guard standing D. Regular drill

38. The word of command "squad lamba dahine - chhota baen" is used for

A. Precise sizing/Kadwar Sizing
B. Movement of squad
C. Separating into two halves
D. Making squad to stand in straight line

39. Teenline banana kise kehte hi/ what will be the action taken If there are more than nine soldiers in a squad?

A. Two files are formed
B. Three files are formed

C. Cadets/Soldiers stand in a single line
D. Cadets/Soldiers stand in a double line

40. Teeno teen kise kehte hi/ What is trio formation?

A. Three soldiers are covering each other from behind in a line
B. Three soldiers are standing side by side
C. Three soldiers are in arc shape
D. None of the above

41. Blank file will always be on which side?

A. Extreme right of the squad
B. Extreme left mostly second file of the squad
C. In the middle of the squad
D. Either side of the squad

Note: If the squad has numbers 11, 14, 17, 20, then there will always be an empty space in the No. 2 file and the middle line from the left. If the squad has numbers 10, 13, 16, 19, then there will be an empty space in the No. 2 file from the left, and in the middle and back line.

42. When is the command "Khuli Line Chal" used?

A. During combat training exercises
B. During VIP inspection in a grand parade
C. During nighttime maneuvers
D. During tactical retreats

43. Distance covered/moved after the word of command "Khuli Line Chal" is________.

    A. 45 Inch
    B. 50 Inch
    C. 30 Inch
    D. 15 Inch Note: Left foot/Baen paon 30inch and Fight foot/Dahine paon 15inch. A total of 45inch covered from the starting point

44. When is the command "Nikat Line Chal" used?

    A. After combat training exercises to move the squad
    B. After nighttime maneuvers to rest the squad
    C. After tactical retreats to move the squad
    D. After VIP inspection in a grand parade

45. In both "Khuli Line Chal" and " Nikat Line Chal" distance covered/moved after the word of command is?

    A. 30inch B. 50inch C. 45inch D. 15inch

46. What is the purpose of "Khade Khade Salute Karna" (Saluting While Standing)?

    A. To greet fellow soldiers and cadets
    B. To show respect to passing officers from nearby you while standing.
    C. To initiate a formal conversation with soldiers
    D. To signal the end of a training session

    Note: If the officers are on the right side it will be "Dahine Salute" If the officers are on the left side it will be "Baen Salute"

47. Identify the correct statements for the "Khade Khade Salute Karna" (Saluting While Standing)?

    I. The fingers and thumb of the right hand are straight and together, the middle finger touching the right eyebrow, one inch to the right of the right eye,
    II. 45-degree angle between the wrist and the elbow
    III. Eyes looking straight ahead, and the rest of the body is in the position of attention.
    IV. The fingers and thumb of the right hand are upright and together, the middle finger touching the fore head
    V. 90-degree angle between the wrist and the elbow

    A. All are correct
    B. I, II and III
    C. III, IV and V
    D. None of these

48. When the word of command "Parade Par" is used?

    A. To dismiss platoon or troops from agitation
    B. To initiate a drill session before ceremonial practice
    C. To bring platoons or troops for a parade from the corner/edge of the parade ground or from their position.
    D. To commence physical training exercises before games

49. Which of the following will play a role as Dahina darshak/Right marker?

    I. Squad commander
    II. Company Havildar Major (CHM)
    III. Platoon Havildar
    IV. Company commander

    A. I, II and III
    B. All of the above
    C. Only IV
    D. Dahine darshak never exist

50. What is the purpose of "Visarjan"? or when will be the word of command "Visarjan" used?

    A. To initiate a new drill session
    B. To dismiss troops when there is no need to fall in again
    C. To conduct an inspection of the troops
    D. To commence a parade again

51. Which of the following is the right procedure of "Visarjan"?

    A. "Turn to the left and salute, take three steps forward and halt, then proceed straight ahead."
    B. "Turn to the back and salute, take three steps forward and halt, then proceed straight ahead."
    C. "Take three steps forward, salute and halt, then proceed straight ahead."
    D. "Turn to the right and salute, take three steps forward and halt, then proceed straight ahead."

52. What is the purpose of "Line Tod"/Breaking line? or when will be the word of command "Line Tod" used?

A. To initiate a new drill session
B. To take a short break and then fall in again
C. To dismiss troops when there is no need to fall in again
D. To conduct an inspection of the troops

Note: 1. The difference between "Visarjan" and Line Tod is - "Saluting is not done during Line Tod" rest every step is same for both.

Rifle Ke Saath Visarjan Aur Line Tod: Action is done in the same way as it is done in empty hand drill, the only difference is that, before dispersal/Visarjan or break Line/Line tod, the rifle is brought into the "Bagal Shastra" position.

53. What is the purpose of "Tez Chal"/"Quick march"?

A. To maintain sequence while moving from one place to another.
B. To conduct physical training exercises and sports
C. To initiate a drill session and end the session
D. To move the squad/platoon/company from one place to another

54. Match the following

Type of marching contingent	Tez Chal steps/Minute
1. regiments/units	P. 110
2. rifle units	Q. 116
3. NCC SD cadets	R. 140

4. NCC SW cadets	S. 120
5. New recruits	T. 135

A. 1P, 2Q, 3,R, 4S, 5T
B. 1Q, 2R, 3S, 4T, 5P
C. 1S, 2R, 3Q, 4P, 5T
D. 1R, 2T, 3Q, 4P, 5S

55. The word of command "Squad tham" is given on ________ foot

A. Left/Baen
B. Right/Dahine
C. Any foot
D. None of these

56. In Tej Chal the distance between cadets is ________ inch

A. 20inch
B. 30inch
C. 45inch
D. 40inch

57. When will be the word of command "Squad tham" is given?

A. When the left foot is on the ground, or the right foot is crossing over the left foot.
B. When the Right foot is on the ground, or the left foot is crossing over the right foot
C. When the both feats are on the ground and resting
D. When the troop is running

58. The word of command "Dhire chal"/Slow march is used during ________

A. Pilots leading the parade walk at a slow pace during VIP inspection
B. All squad walking a slow pace during ceremonial drill

C. Only VIP and parade commander walking slowly
D. Drill test during B and C certificate exam

Note: Dhire chal is also done during Passing out parade

59. Length and pace of steps during "Dhire chal"/ slow march is________.

A. Length of each step is 20inches and the pace is 60 steps/minute
B. Length of each step is 40inches and the pace is 70steps/minute
C. Length of each step is 30inches and the pace is 70steps/minute
D. Length of each step is 25inches and the pace is 55steps/minute

60. What is word of command used "if the gap between the rightmost squad and the adjacent squad on the right side is more, then the action of taking right steps is carried out to adjust it".

A. "Dahine Baju Kadam Lena" (Taking Right side steps)
B. "Baen Baju Kadam Lena" (Taking Left side steps)
C. "Aage Kadam Lena" (Taking forward steps)
D. "Piche Kadam Lena" (Taking backward steps

61. Which of the following word of command is used "When the gap between the leftmost squad and the adjacent squad on the left side has increased while standing still, the action of taking left steps is carried out to adjust it".

   A. "Dahine Baju Kadam Lena" (Taking Right side steps)
   B. "Baen Baju Kadam Lena" (Taking Left side steps)
   C. "Aage Kadam Lena" (Taking forward steps)
   D. "Piche Kadam Lena" (Taking backward steps

62. Which of the following word of command is used "When there is a slightly greater distance between one squad and the next while standing still, the action of taking forward steps is carried out to adjust the distance"?

   A. "Dahine Baju Kadam Lena" (Taking Right side steps)
   B. "Baen Baju Kadam Lena" (Taking Left side steps)
   C. "Aage Kadam Lena" (Taking forward steps)
   D. "Piche Kadam Lena" (Taking backward steps

63. Which of the following word of command is used "When there is a slightly greater distance between one squad and the previous squad while standing still, the action of taking backward steps is carried out to adjust the distance"?

   A. "Dahine Baju Kadam Lena" (Taking Right side steps)
   B. "Baen Baju Kadam Lena" (Taking Left side steps)
   C. "Aage Kadam Lena" (Taking forward steps)
   D. "Piche Kadam Lena" (Taking backward steps)

64. What is the minimum and maximum steps taken while performing Dahine Baju Kadam Lena" (Taking Right side steps) or "Baen Baju Kadam Lena" (Taking Left side steps)?

A. 4 steps and up to 12 steps
B. 3[st]eps and up to 9[st]eps
C. 5 steps and up to 15 steps
D. No restriction of steps

NOTE: When standing still, if the gap between the rightmost squad and the adjacent squad on the right side is more, then the action of taking "right step" is carried out to adjust it. The length of each step is 12 inches, and as per the word of command, right steps can be taken up to 4 steps. This continues until 12 steps. If the gap is still more, then it is completed by turning to the right.

65. Match the following

Tez Chal Se Mudna/ Salute	Action taken
1. Tez Chal Se Dahine Mudna	P. Turning 180°
2. Tez Chal Se Baen Mudna	Q. Turning 90° left
3. Tez Chal Se Piche Mudna	R. Officers and JCOs in front of you
4. Tez Chal Se Samne Salute Karna	S. Officers on your right side

5. Tez Chal Se Dahine Salute Karna	T. Officers on your left side
6. Tez Chal Se Baen Salute Karna	U. Turning 90° right

A. 1U, 2Q, 3P, 4R, 5S, 6T
B. 1P,2Q, 3U, 4R, 5S, 6T
C. 1U,2P, 3Q, 4T, 5S, 6R
D. 1Q, 2U, 3 P, 4S, 5R, 6T

66. What is "Teenon Teen Se Ek File Banana" (Creating a File from Three to One)?

A. To increase the number of files during a march.
B. To decrease the number of cadets during a parade
C. To navigate through narrow paths, bridges, or to moving into a lecture hall with three people abreast by forming a single file.
D. To disperse the parade and signal the end of a training session

67. What is "Ek File Se Teenon Teen Banana" (Converting a single row from One to Three)?

A. To increase the number of files during a march.
B. To decrease the number of cadets during a parade
C. After completion of navigation through narrow paths, bridges, or coming out from a lecture hall in single line abreast by forming a three file.
D. To disperse the parade and signal the end of a training session

68. Match the following for rifle drill

Commands of Rifle drill	Action done
1. Bhumi Shastra	P. Bagal Shastra se rifle ko niche lane ke liye, Parade samapti hone ke bad bhi Bagal Shastra se rifle niche lane ke liye karyawahi karte hain.
2. Uthao Shastra	Q. Rifle ke saath ek jagah se dusri jagah jana ho to, regiment / unit contingent march past karke jaate hain. Quarter guard mein khada sentry Nb/Sub se Captain tak ko, bagal shastra se salute karta hai.
3. Bagal Shastra	R. Jab rifle ko savdhan position se zamin se uthana ho toh
4. Baju Shastra	S. guard of honour mein VIP ko izzat dene ke liye aur quarter guard mein khara sentry, Major se upar wale Officer ko izzat dene ke liye Salami Shastra ki karyawahi karta hai.
5. Salami Shastra	T. Jab rifle ko savdhan position se zamin pe rakhna ho to

A. 1P, 2Q, 3R, 4S, 5T
B. 1Q, 2R, 3P, 4S, 5T
C. 1T, 2S, 3R, 4Q, 5P
D. 1T, 2R, 3Q, 4P, 5S

69. "Salami Shastra" is given to ________

A. All officers of defense
B. All civil administrators
C. Major and above ranks
D. All martyrs

70. "Bagal Shastra" is given to ________

A. Naib Subedar to Captain ranks
B. All civil administrators
C. Major and above ranks
D. All martyrs

71. How many soldiers are required for "Guard Mounting"?

A. 5+6 B. 3+4 C. 5+2 D. 6+2

72. What is the purpose of "Guard Mounting"?

A. Conducting a drill session
B. Cleaning of weapons and maintain records
C. For security at the Quarter Guard and also respecting any authorized officer's during visit to the unit
D. Checking Identity cards and doing sentry duty at the entrance

73. For Guard mounting procedure, fall in will be in ________ ranks.

A. 2 B. 3 C. 4 D. 1

74. Which of the following is correct for "Guard mounting"?

A. 6 Jawans, 1 Guard commander and 1Guard 2IC
B. 5 Jawans, 1 Guard commander and 2 Guard 2IC

C. Only 8 Jawans will be there

D. 4 Jawans, 2 Guard commander and 2 Guard 2IC

75. In "Guard mounting Guard commander will always stands on which side of Guard?

A. Left

B. In the Middle

C. Right

D. Back

76. What is the strength of Guard of Honour for president?

A. 150 rank and file

B. 100 rank and file

C. 120 rank and file

D. 130 rank and file

77. What is the strength of Guard of Honour for Vice President and Prime Minister?

A. 150 rank and file

B. 130 rank and file

C. 100 rank and file

D. 120 rank and file

78. Which of the following officers are entitled for "General Salute"?

A. Only to President

B. Colonel and above ranks

C. Major General and above ranks

D. Only to Chief of Army staff

79. National Salute/Rashtriya Salute is given to ________

A. President and Governors of the state

B. Prime minister

C. Major General and above ranks

D. War martyrs

80. Who are entitled for Salami Shastra.
    1. Major and above ranks
    2. To all VIPs.
    3. All army officers
    4. University Vice chancellors

A. 1 and 3
B. 3 and 4
C. 1,2 and 3
D. 1,2 and 4

81. In Guard of Honour, "The guard will form up in _________, with a distance of four paces/4kadam between the front/Agli line and rear lines/Pichli.

A. Two ranks
B. Three ranks
C. 4. Four ranks
D. Five ranks

82. There are how many types of salutes?

A. 1
B. 2
C. 3
D. 4

83. With weapon and without weapon, there are how many types of salutes?

A. 3
B. 2
C. 5
D. 6

84. What is rank and what is file?

A. Standing side by side in a row and File is standing in 3s in a column
B. Standing side by side in a column and File is standing in 3s in a row
C. Standing in zig-zag in rank and File is standing in a rows
D. Standing side by side in a row and File is standing in 3s in zig-zag

85. Match the following: Squad and its strength

Type of squad	Number/Strength
I. RDC Contingent	A. 30
II. Platoon	B. 10
III. Company (Coy)	C. 160
IV. Troop	D. 100
V. Section	E. 110

A. IE, IID, IIIC, IVB, VA
B. IE, IIA, IIIC, IVD, VB
C. IA, IIB, IIIC, IVD, VE
D. IB, IIC, IIIA, IVD, VE

86. How many steps one has to move in "Samiksha kram"?

A. 13 Khali Ek Do
B. 14 Khali Ek Do
C. 12 Kali Ek Do
D. 16 Khali Ek Do

1. A	2. B	3. C	4. A	5. B	6. A	7. C	8. C	9. B	10. B
11. A	12. C	13. B	14. A	15. C	16. D	17. B	18. C	19. A	20. B
21. B	22. B	23. B	24. C	25. B	26. A	27. B	28. D	29. A	30. C
31. C	32. B	33. D	34. B	35. D	36. C	37. A	38. A	39. B	40. A
41. B	42. B	43. A	44. D	45. C	46. B	47. B	48. C	49. A	50. B
51. D	52. B	53. D	54. C	55. A	56. B	57. A	58. A	59. C	60. A
61. B	62. C	63. D	64. A	65. A	66. C	67. C	68. D	69.C	70. A
71. D	72. C	73. A	74. A	75. C	76. A	77. C	78. C	79. A	80. D
81. A	82. C	83. D	84. A	85. B	86. A				

04

Weapon Training

4.1 INTRODUCTION TO .22 RIFLE

1. What is the primary use of the.22 rifle for NCC cadets?

   A. For hunting
   B. To increase physical fitness
   C. To practice shooting
   D. For decoration

2. What is the length of the.22 Rifle No II MK IV BA?

   A. 43 inches
   B. 40 inches
   C. 50 inches
   D. 45 inches

3. The magazine capacity of of.22 Rifle and.22 Deluxe BA hold?

   A. 5 rounds
   B. 10 rounds
   C. 15 rounds
   D. 20 rounds

4. What is the muzzle velocity of the.22 Rifle and.22 Deluxe BA?

   A. 3000 feet per second
   B. 2700 feet per second
   C. 2500 feet per second
   D. 3200 feet per second

5. What is the effective range of the.22 Rifle?

   A. 25 yards
   B. 10 yards
   C. 50 yards
   D. 100 yards

6. The maximum range of.22 Rifle at a 33-degree angle is approximately?

   A. 1000 yards C. 1700 yards
   B. 1500 yards D. 2000 yards

7. How many grooves are there in the barrel of the Point 22 rifle?

   A. 4 B. 6 C. 8 D. 10

8. What is the rate of fire during rapid firing for the Point 22 rifle?

   A. 10-15 rounds/min C. 5-10 rounds/min
   B. 15-20 rounds/min D. 20-25 rounds/min

9. What type of bullet does the Point 22 rifle use?

   A. Copper C. Plastic
   B. Lead/Copper D. Rubber

10. What is the weight of the Rifle Point 22 Deluxe BA?

    A. 3.93 kg B. 2.78 kg C. 4.5 kg D. 1.5 kg

11. What is the length of the Point 22 bullet with its case?

    A. 10 mm B. 12 mm C. 15 mm D. 20 mm

12. What is the calibre of the Point 22 rifle?

    A. 0.30 inches C. 0.22 inches
    B. 0.25 inches D. 0.50 inches

13. Which of the following describes rimmed ammunition?

    A. Bullet with no rim C. Bullet with plastic coating
    B. None of the above D. Bullet with a visible rim

14. Which part of the rifle is removed first when disassembling?

    A. Sling
    B. Bayonet
    C. Safety catch
    D. Bolt

15. What is the last component fitted during reassembling the rifle?

    A. Bolt
    B. Trigger
    C. Bayonet
    D. Sling

16. Where should the sling be placed after removing it from the rifle?

    A. On the table
    B. Hung on the wall
    C. Rolled and placed on a ground sheet
    D. Placed inside the magazine

17. When disassembling the rifle, safety catch must be placed at ________ position.

    A. S
    B. F
    C. R
    D. T

18. What is the purpose of sight setting on the rifle?

    A. To increase the firing speed
    B. To adjust the range
    C. To reduce recoil
    D. To clean the rifle

19. What type of cleaning is performed daily on the rifle?

    A. Full cleaning
    B. Dusting
    C. Oil change
    D. Greasing

20. How often should the rifle undergo a quarterly cleaning?

    A. Every 1-month
    B. Every 6 months
    C. Every year
    D. Every 3 months

21. Who inspects the rifle during firing practice?

    A. The shooter
    B. The instructor
    C. The armourer
    D. The squad leader

22. What is the size of the cleaning cloth (chindi) for regular cleaning?

    A. 4x1 inch
    B. 5x2 inch
    C. 3x1 inch
    D. 4x1.5 inch

23. How should the barrel of the rifle be cleaned after firing?

    A. Using cold water
    B. Using warm water
    C. Using oil only
    D. No cleaning required

24. What is the weight of the Point 22 bullet?

    A. 20-25 grams
    B. 30-35 grams
    C. 38-40 grams
    D. 45-50 grams

25. What should be done if multiple rifles are disassembled simultaneously?

    A. Parts can be mixed
    B. Use new parts
    C. Check the registration numbers
    D. Leave them disassembled

1. C	2. D	3. A	4. B	5. A	6. C	7. B	8. A	9. B	10. B
11. C	12. C	13. D	14. B	15. C	16. C	17. A	18. B	19. B	20. D
21. C	22. D	23. B	24. C	25. C					

4.2 HANDLING OF .22 RIFLE

1. What is a key quality of a good firer?

   A. Accuracy in aiming
   B. Strength
   C. Quick loading and firing
   D. Communication skills

2. How is ammunition loaded into the Point 22 Deluxe Rifle?

   A. Using a charger
   B. Through a belt feed system
   C. Automatically
   D. One by one into the magazine

3. What is the first step in loading a Point 22 rifle while lying down?

   A. Take a long step with the left foot
   B. Pull the trigger
   C. Cock the bolt
   D. Fire a round

4. What should be done to unload the rifle?

   A. Push the bolt forward
   B. Press the trigger
   C. Pull the bolt back to eject the round
   D. Shake the rifle

5. Why lying position is important in shooting?

   A. It reduces fatigue
   B. It creates a small profile, making it harder for the enemy to see

C. It increases shooting range
D. It allows for faster movement

6. Which of the following is important while taking a lying position?

A. Ensure both legs are closed
B. Keep your left elbow in line with the targe
C. Place the right hand above the rifle
D. Avoid using the left hand

7. What part of the hand holds the rifle during proper holding?

A. Wrist
B. The 'V' between the thumb and index finger
C. Thumb
D. Palm only

8. What is crucial for maintaining a firm grip on the rifle?

A. Keeping both elbows off the ground
B. Holding the barrel
C. Using only one hand
D. Ensuring the left elbow is stable on the ground

9. How should the trigger be operated for accurate shooting?

A. Use the index finger and apply pressure gradually
B. Quickly pull the trigger
C. Use the middle finger
D. Tap the trigger repeatedly

10. What happens if the rifle barrel moves while pressing the trigger?

    A. The shot will be accurate
    B. The rifle will jam
    C. The bullet may miss the target
    D. Nothing happens

11. What should a shooter do after the first trigger pull?

    A. Stop breathing momentarily
    B. Change position
    C. Move their head
    D. Press the trigger hard

12. What is the purpose of the "disk test" in trigger operation?

    A. To check rifle weight
    B. To test firing speed
    C. To ensure the barrel does not move during trigger press
    D. To check the ammunition

13. How should a shooter maintain their focus while firing?

    A. Focus on the entire rifle
    B. Look around for targets
    C. Focus on the foresight tip
    D. Focus on the ground

14. What is the purpose of checking sight picture after trigger pull?

    A. To reset the rifle
    B. To load the next round

C. To confirm the shot's direction
D. To adjust the scope

15. What does "follow through" refer to in shooting?

A. Calling out the target after firing
B. Adjusting the rifle's scope
C. Resetting the rifle for the next shot
D. Leaving the shooting position

16. What should be done before loading the Point 22 rifle?

A. Clean the ammunition
B. Adjust the sight
C. Check the trigger
D. Remove the bolt

17. How is the body adjusted in the lying position to remove tension?

A. Move the legs side to side
B. Adjust the elbow and body back and forth
C. Raise the head
D. Bend the knees

18. When should the rifle be loaded, cocked, and unloaded?

A. Anytime
B. While running
C. Only when given a command
D. During cleaning

19. What part of the hand should be placed under the handguard for stability?

A. Thumb
B. Index finger
C. Palm
D. Forearm

20. Which part of the body is crucial in adjusting the rifle's alignment while shooting?

    A. Right foot
    B. Left knee
    C. Left shoulder
    D. Right elbow

21. Where should the left elbow be placed in relation to the body while holding the rifle?

    A. Directly in front of the knee
    B. In a straight line with the left shoulder
    C. Behind the body
    D. Resting on the hip

22. How should the rifle's fore sight tip move while aiming?

    A. From left to right
    B. Back and forth
    C. It should not move at all
    D. Up and down between the 6 and 12 o'clock positions

23. What should be done if the rifle points too far left during shooting?

    A. Push the rifle down
    B. Stand up and reposition
    C. Adjust the right foot to the left
    D. Move the target

24. What should be done if the rifle points too high?

    A. Push the right-hand forward
    B. Adjust the sight
    C. Pull the rifle back
    D. Lower the barrel

25. What should you focus on during the final trigger pull for a shot?

    A. The target's size
    B. The alignment of the foresight tip with the point of aim
    C. The rifle's weight
    D. The sound of the bullet

1. C	2. D	3. A	4. C	5. B	6. B	7. B	8. D	9. A	10. C
11. A	12. C	13. C	14. C	15. A	16. A	17. B	18. C	19. C	20. D
21. B	22. D	23. C	24. A	25. B					

4.3 RANGE PROCEDURE AND THEORY OF GROUP

1. What is the primary purpose of conducting shooting practice on a range?

   A. To build physical strength
   B. For entertainment
   C. To maintain shooting skills
   D. To improve communication

2. Which of the following is not part of the preparations before firing on the range?

   A. Placing a red flag on the stop butt
   B. Ensuring soft soil without stones in the stop butt
   C. Using a scope
   D. Arranging a firing point register

3. What is the height of the staff pole on the right side of the stop butt?

   A. 20 feet B. 10 feet C. 15 feet D. 25 feet

4. What should be placed 12 feet from the markers gallery?

   A. White flag
   B. Target plate
   C. Pole
   D. Red flag

5. Which document is needed for range clearance before firing?

   A. Firing point register
   B. Ammunition details
   C. Lead deposit certificate
   D. Range standing orders

6. Who ensures the safety and readiness of the ammunition before firing?

   A. Armourer
   B. Firer
   C. Instructor
   D. Coach

7. What is the purpose of the "butt party"?

   A. Cleaning weapons
   B. Managing communication
   C. Controlling targets
   D. Collecting ammunition

8. What is the minimum number of rounds fired to form a "group"?

   A. 3
   B. 5
   C. 7
   D. 10

9. What does "MPI" stand for in group firing?

   A. Mean Precision Index
   B. Maximum Point Interval
   C. Mean Point of Impact
   D. Military Precision Indicator

10. What should be done if the MPI is off from the Point of Aim (POA)?

A. Zero the weapon
B. Change the target
C. Stop firing
D. Fire more rounds

11. Which is more important in firing?

A. Speed
B. Accuracy
C. Ammunition type
D. Target size

12. How is a firer's grouping capacity measured?

A. By the number of bullets fired
B. By the range distance
C. By the weight of the bullets
D. By the size of the group in inches

13. What is the maximum number of bullets a cadet fires in the Advanced Shooting Competition?

A. 15 B. 20 C. 25 D. 30

14. What is the first step in the lying position during the Advanced Shooting Competition?

A. Adjust the target
B. Reload the rifle
C. Fire 5 bullets for sight setting
D. Move to the standing position

15. How many bullets are fired in the kneeling position during the Advanced Shooting Competition?

A. 5 B. 10 C. 15 D. 20

16. In the standing position of the Advanced Shooting Competition, how many bullets are fired for sight setting?

    A. 3 B. 5 C. 10 D. 15

17. What is the maximum score achievable in the Advanced Shooting Competition?

    A. 20 B. 25 C. 30 D. 35

18. What is the purpose of "sight setting"?

    A. To change the target
    B. To increase the number of rounds fired
    C. To adjust the rifle's alignment for accuracy
    D. To test the ammunition

19. What is the basic principle emphasized in shooting?

    A. "One bullet, one enemy"
    B. "Shoot and reload"
    C. "Faster is better"
    D. "Focus on movement"

20. What should a firer ensure before leaving the firing point?

    A. Clean the rifle
    B. Clear the weapon and check safety devices
    C. Aim at a new target
    D. Reload the weapon

21. What is the role of the "nominal roll"?

    A. List the weapons used
    B. Track the ammunition count

C. Record the names of the firers
D. Record the target numbers

22. What is used to blacken the foresight during shooting practice?

A. Charcoal
B. Marker pen
C. Black paint
D. Foresight blanking point

23. What is the key to good grouping in firing?

A. Speed of reloading
B. Adjusting the target after every shot
C. Maintaining the correct position
D. Switching rifles frequently

24. Who is responsible for issuing ammunition during range practice?

A. The firer
B. The ammunition collection detail
C. The coach
D. The target group

25. What should be done if there is a malfunction during firing?

A. Continue firing
B. Change the target
C. Immediately stop firing and follow safety protocols
D. Increase firing speed

1. C	2. C	3. A	4. D	5. D	6. A	7. C	8. B	9. C	10. A
11. B	12. D	13. D	14. C	15. B	16. B	17. B	18. C	19. A	20. B
21. C	22. D	23. C	24. B	25. C					

4.4 SHORT RANGE FIRING

1. How many rounds are authorized per cadet during short-range firing?

   A. 10 B. 12 C. 14 D. 15

2. How many rounds are pooled for zeroing and reclassification of failures?

   A. 1 B. 2 C. 3 D. 4

3. What action should be taken if the bullet hits above or below the point of aim despite correct aiming?

   A. Fire again
   B. Change the target
   C. Adjust the back sight
   D. Clean the rifle

4. What is the effect of altering the sight by 50 yards?

   A. The effect halves
   B. No effect
   C. The effect doubles
   D. The effect triples

5. How much does the mean point of impact (MPI) rise or drop at 300 yards?

   A. 6 inches
   B. 12 inches
   C. 18 inches
   D. 24 inches

6. Which position is recommended for deliberate firing at 25 yards?

   A. Standing unsupported
   B. Lying supported
   C. Sitting supported
   D. Kneeling unsupported

7. How many rounds are fired in one practice session of deliberate firing?

   A. 3 B. 5 C. 7 D. 10

8. What is the maximum score for hitting the bull and inner targets?

   A. 1 point B. 2 points C. 3 points D. 4 points

9. What is the scoring for hitting the outer target?

   A. 1 point B. 2 points C. 3 points D. 4 points

10. What is the main goal of short-range firing at the range?

    A. To learn the anatomy of the rifle
    B. To practice hand-to-hand combat
    C. To clean the rifle
    D. To improve self-protection skills

11. Which rifle model is used for short-range firing?

    A. Rifle.22 No MK-II
    B. Rifle.25 MK-I
    C. Rifle.22 MK-III
    D. Rifle.30 MK-IV

12. What is critical for a rifle's efficiency besides cleaning and maintenance?

    A. Weight of the rifle
    B. Firer's skill
    C. Type of ammunition
    D. Length of the barrel

13. Which position is described as the best for accurate firing?

    A. Sitting
    B. Standing
    C. Lying
    D. Kneeling

14. What is the target size used for short-range firing at 25 yards?

    A. 2' x 2'
    B. 1' x 1'
    C. 3' x 3'
    D. 4' x 4'

15. What are the three basic principles of accurate firing?

    A. Strong grip, sighting, and trigger control
    B. Weak grip, sighting, and reloading
    C. Fast grip, aiming, and firing
    D. Strong grip, aiming, and rapid fire

16. What is necessary to ensure safe and accurate firing?

    A. Following proper range procedure
    B. Standing close to the target
    C. Having an assistant
    D. Firing rapidly

17. What is sight alteration used for?

    A. Increasing the range
    B. Adjusting the bullet to the point of aim
    C. Focusing on distant objects
    D. Cleaning the rifle sight

18. What is the recommended action before starting firing?

    A. Clean the rifle
    B. Adjust the scope
    C. Follow all orders and instructions
    D. Choose a new target

19. How much does the MPI rise or drop at 400 yards?

A. 6 inches
B. 12 inches
C. 18 inches
D. 24 inches

20. What happens if sight alteration is made at 200 yards?

A. The effect doubles
B. No effect
C. The effect halves
D. The effect triples

1. B	2. B	3. C	4. A	5. B	6. B	7. B	8. C	9. A	10. D
11. A	12. B	13. C	14. B	15. A	16. A	17. B	18. C	19. C	20. A

05

Personality Development

1. What makes an individual's personality unique from others?

   A. Physical appearance
   B. Mental characteristics
   C. Financial status
   D. Age

2. Why personality development is important?

   A. To create a strong positive impression
   B. To make more money
   C. To travel more
   D. To become famous

3. How skills are acquired?

   A. Instantly
   B. Through practice and patience
   C. By luck
   D. By birth

4. What is the benefit of being a skilled person?

   A. Uses less time, energy, and resources
   B. Earns more money
   C. Becomes popular
   D. Travels a lot

5. According to WHO, what are life skills?

   A. Abilities for adopting positive behavior
   B. Techniques for cooking

C. Skills for making money
D. Methods for traveling

6. Which of the following is self-awareness?

   A. Recognition of self, character, strengths, and weaknesses
   B. Ignoring one's weaknesses
   C. Only focusing on strengths
   D. Comparing oneself to others

7. What is empathy?

   A. Being sensitive to another person's situation
   B. Ignoring others' feelings
   C. Focusing only on oneself
   D. Avoiding emotions

8. What is critical thinking?

   A. Accepting all information without questioning
   B. Ignoring facts
   C. Following others' opinions
   D. The ability to analyze information objectively

9. How creative thinking helps?

   A. To generate new ideas by combining existing ideas
   B. To avoid creativity
   C. To stick to traditional methods
   D. To follow others' ideas

10. What do you mean by problem-solving skills?

    A. Identifying the problem and deciding on the best solution
    B. Ignoring problems
    C. Complaining about problems
    D. Avoiding solutions

11. What is decision making?

    A. Following others' decisions
    B. Choosing from varied options based on knowledge
    C. Making random choices
    D. Ignoring options

12. The ability of establishing a positive relationship with other is called________.

    A. Avoiding people
    B. Ignoring relationships
    C. Interpersonal relationship
    D. Focusing on oneself

13. What is effective communication?

    A. The ability to express oneself verbally and non-verbally
    B. Only writing
    C. Speaking without thinking
    D. Avoiding gestures

14. Coping with emotions means_________.

    A. Being aware of predominant emotions and responding appropriately
    B. Ignoring emotions

C. Always being happy
D. Avoiding emotional situations

15. What does coping with stress mean?

A. Recognizing the source of stress and acting to control it
B. Ignoring stress
C. Complaining about stress
D. Avoiding all stressful situations

1. B	2. A	3. B	4. A	5. A	6. A	7. A	8. D	9. A	10. A
11. B	12. C	13. A	14. A	15. A					

5.1 FACTORS INFLUENCING / SHAPING PERSONALITY

1. Based on psychological studies which of the following factors is suggested to have a lasting effect on personality?

A. Diet
B. Wealth
C. Family and Friends
D. Heredity, environment, and education

2. _________ influence your personality through heredity.

A. The weather
B. Daily routine
C. Favourite food
D. Inherited genes from parents

3. Apart from physical attributes, what else influences personality?

   A. Skills
   B. Mental aptitudes and temperaments
   C. Wealth
   D. Clothing style

4. What is the most important factor that influences one's personality?

   A. Self-development
   B. Wealth
   C. Hobbies
   D. Favourite colour

5. The key character to self-development is_______.

   A. Ignoring weaknesses
   B. Believing in oneself and one's capabilities
   C. Avoiding challenges
   D. Following others

6. How does the environment influence our personality?

   A. By determining our physical appearance
   B. Only during adulthood
   C. By influencing our dreams
   D. Through home, family, school, friends, and culture

7. Who are "school smarts"?

   A. Learning from experiences
   B. Knowledge gained from school
   C. Practical skills
   D. Life experiences

8. Which of the following affect our personality in varying degrees?

   A. Life-situations
   C. Favourite books
   B. Fashion trends
   D. Television shows

9. ________ positively influence our personality in life situations.

   A. Ignoring challenges
   B. Competence in handling
   C. Complaining about problems
   D. Avoiding experiences

10. How do dreams and ambitions shape our personality?

    A. By determining our physical appearance
    B. By facilitating our goals and setting priorities
    C. By influencing our diet
    D. By changing our height

11. What do you mean by self-image?

    A. Wealth
    B. Physical strength
    C. Personality characteristics
    D. Eating habits

12. ________ greatly influences the personality of an individual.

    A. Hobbies
    B. Values a person strongly believes in
    C. Physical appearance
    D. Favourite sports

1. D	2. D	3. B	4. A	5. B	6. D	7. B	8. A	9. B	10. B	11. C	12. B

5.2 SELF AWARENESS

1. What is self-awareness?

   A. Knowing our strengths only
   B. Ignoring our weaknesses
   C. Knowing ourselves and our personality
   D. Comparing ourselves to others

2. Self-awareness includes ________

   A. Thoughts, emotions, likes, dislikes, strengths, and weaknesses
   B. Favourite foods
   C. Physical appearance only
   D. Financial status

3. What are the two aspects to concentrate on self-awareness?

   A. How we perceive ourselves and how others perceive us
   B. Our physical appearance and our age
   C. Our wealth and our social status
   D. Our hobbies and our skills

4. Which of the following is NOT one of the three aspects of self-perception?

   A. The perceive self
   B. The ideal self
   C. The real self
   D. The imaginary self

5. What causes unhappiness and poor adjustments in people?

   A. Having too many hobbies
   B. Discrepancies between the perceived and the real or ideal self

C. Focusing only on strengths
D. Being overly happy

1. C	2. A	3. A	4. D	5. B

5.3 EMPATHY

1. What happens to communication without empathy?

   A. It becomes more effective
   B. It becomes one-sided and faces problems
   C. It remains the same
   D. It improves significantly

2. Which of the following is a component of empathy?

   A. Ignoring the other person's feelings
   B. Putting oneself in the other's shoes
   C. Agreeing with the person no matter what
   D. Taking the issue on one's own shoulders

3. What is being non-judgmental means?

   A. Agreeing or disagreeing with the person
   B. Accepting the person and their behaviour without judgment
   C. Ignoring the person's feelings
   D. Taking the issue personally

1. B	2. B	3. B

5.4 DECISION MAKING AND PROBLEM SOLVING

1. We often take decisions most likely based on_______.

   A. Future experiences
   B. Random choices
   C. Past experiences
   D. Other people's decisions

2. The essential quality required for good decision-making is________.

   A. Ignoring the situation
   B. Avoiding visualization of consequences
   C. Making decisions hastily
   D. Understanding the situation well

3. What should we do first to solve a problem effectively?

   A. Ignore the problem
   B. Think about the problem only
   C. Write down the problem on paper
   D. Escape from the problem

4. Problem solving or talking problems help us to develop_________.

   A. Fear of new issues
   B. Our skills and potentials
   C. Mental stress
   D. Evasion techniques

5. Which is a minor decision?

   A. What career to choose
   B. Where to buy a house
   C. When and whom to marry
   D. What to eat

1. C	2. D	3. C	4. B	5. D

5.5 CRITICAL AND CREATIVE THINKING

1. What is critical thinking?

   A. Accepting all information as true
   B. Determining the authenticity, accuracy, or value of something
   C. Ignoring logical reasoning
   D. Making quick decisions without analysis

2. Critical thinking includes skills such as ________

   A. Ignoring alternatives
   B. Accepting all perspectives
   C. Comparing and classifying
   D. Avoiding logical reasoning

3. Which of the following is NOT a characteristic of critical thinking?

   A. Seeking reasons and alternatives
   B. Perceiving the total situation
   C. Changing one's views based on evidence
   D. Ignoring evidence

4. Critical thinking requires skills in_________.

   A. Analyzing information and examining it in detail
   B. Ignoring different perspectives
   C. Making decisions without considering information
   D. Avoiding logical reasoning

5. What does open-mindedness in critical thinking mean?

   A. Sticking to one point of view
   B. Examining multiple points of view
   C. Ignoring other opinions
   D. Being inflexible

6. What is creativity?

   A. The ability to generate new ideas by combining, changing, or reapplying existing ideas
   B. The ability to create something out of nothing
   C. Avoiding new ideas
   D. Ignoring practical solutions

7. Which of the following is an attitude of creativity?

   A. Rejecting change and newness
   B. Accepting change and newness
   C. Avoiding flexibility
   D. Ignoring possibilities

8. Which of the following is a characteristic feature of a creative person?

   A. Avoiding challenges
   B. Ignoring problems
   C. Enjoying challenges
   D. Giving up easily

9. Creative people work hard to__________.

   A. Avoid improving ideas and solutions
   B. Improve ideas and solutions continuously
   C. Produce works of excellence with one stroke of brilliance
   D. Ignore gradual alterations and refinements

10. What does it mean for a creative person to challenge assumptions?

    A. Accepting all assumptions without question
    B. Questioning and testing existing beliefs and ideas
    C. Avoiding curiosity
    D. Ignoring problems

1. B	2. C	3. D	4. A	5. B	6. A	7. B	8. C	9. B	10. B

5.6 COMMUNICATION SKILLS

1. What is communication?

   A. Sharing ideas, opinions, thoughts and feelings,
   B. Keeping thoughts and feelings to oneself
   C. Only talking to people, you know
   D. Avoiding interaction with others

2. What happens if we do not talk with others?

   A. They will understand us
   B. We will feel lonely
   C. Communication will improve
   D. Misunderstandings will decrease

3. The lack of communication in relationships lead to__________.

   A. Better understanding
   B. Stronger relationships
   C. Problems and misunderstandings
   D. Increased empathy

4. Which communication style believes they are always right?

   A. Aggressive
   B. Passive
   C. Assertive
   D. None of the above

5. Which communication style does not express true feelings and always agrees with others?

   A. Aggressive
   B. Passive
   C. Assertive
   D. None of the above

6. Which communication style believes that both they and others are valuable?

   A. Aggressive
   B. Passive
   C. Assertive
   D. None of the above

7. What does verbal communication involves?

   A. Writing letters
   B. Using body language only
   C. Talking and listening
   D. Ignoring the speaker

8. What is an example of non-verbal communication?

   A. Speaking loudly
   B. Nodding or smiling
   C. Writing a letter
   D. Reading a book

9. What can help to reduce the communication gap?

   A. Ignoring others
   B. Speaking vaguely
   C. Planning ahead
   D. Avoiding feedback

10. What is important for effective listening during communication?

    A. Interrupting the speaker
    B. Not paying attention
    C. Giving attention to all that is said without interrupting
    D. Only focusing on points relevant to oneself

11. Which of the following is a listening barrier?

    A. Clear message
    B. Not maintaining eye contact with the speaker
    C. Good understanding of the receiver
    D. Speaking clearly

12. Which of the following is a barrier while speaking?

    A. Clear message
    B. Consistency in communication
    C. Incomplete sentences or mumbling
    D. Good eye contact

13. Which of the following is another barrier to effective communication?

    A. Listening carefully
    B. Assumptions
    C. Speaking clearly
    D. Understanding the receiver

14. What is important to observe in others to reduce the communication gap?

    A. Their clothes
    B. Their handwriting
    C. Their body language or non-verbal communication
    D. Their personal interests

15. Which of the following is NOT a way of communication?

    A. Aggressive
    B. Passive
    C. Assertive
    D. Defensive

1. A	2. B	3. C	4. A	5. B	6. C	7. C	8. B	9. C	10. C
11. B	12. C	13. B	14. C	15. D					

5.7 GROUP DISCUSSIONS, COPING WITH STRESS AND EMOTIONS

1. What is stress?

   A. A rare phenomenon
   B. Always a negative thing
   C. Our body's reaction to people and events
   D. Never helpful

2. Too much stress results in ________.

   A. Happiness
   B. Lower self-esteem
   C. Improved health
   D. Increased energy

3. What is the first step in coping with stress?

   A. Ignoring it
   B. Recognizing the source of stress
   C. Blaming others
   D. Avoiding responsibilities

4. Taking deep breaths help in________.

   A. Increasing stress
   B. Reducing stress
   C. Staying awake
   D. Feeling more angry

5. Which physical activity reduce stress?

   A. Running
   B. Sitting still
   C. Watching TV
   D. Eating junk food

6. What should you do when making a schedule?

   A. Include time for stress reduction
   B. Make unrealistic plans
   C. Ignore your tasks
   D. Do everything at once

7. How can you deal with a problem beyond your control?

   A. Ignore it completely
   B. Blame others
   C. Worry constantly
   D. Accept it as it is for now

1. C	2. B	3. B	4. B	5. A	6. A	7. D

5.8 CHANGE MIND SET

1. What does a mindset include?

   A. Only your thoughts about others
   B. Your knowledge, beliefs, and thoughts about the world and yourself
   C. Only your emotions
   D. None of the above

2. How can you identify self-limiting beliefs?

   A. By examining your current beliefs and asking the right questions
   B. By blaming others
   C. By avoiding self-reflection
   D. By ignoring them

3. What is the benefit of having a clear vision and goals?

   A. It shapes your mindset to achieve your vision
   B. It creates confusion
   C. It makes you feel overwhelmed
   D. It discourages personal growth

4. How can you protect your mindset?

   A. By ignoring your goals
   B. By avoiding negative influences and staying confident
   C. By listening to everyone's opinions
   D. By constantly comparing yourself to others

5. What should you avoid to maintain a positive mindset?

   A. Setting personal goals
   B. Being grateful for your successes
   C. Making comparisons with others
   D. Focusing on your own needs

6. How should you redefine failure?

   A. As the end of the journey
   B. As something to avoid at all costs
   C. As a reason to stop trying
   D. As a lesson learned

1. B	2. A	3. A	4. B	5. C	6. D

5.9 TIME MANAGEMENT

1. What is the aim of time management?

   A. To accomplish everything, you want to do
   B. To prioritize tasks and use limited time effectively
   C. To eliminate all stress from your life
   D. To remember all tasks without any tools

2. Which of the following is NOT a benefit of time management?

   A. Reducing wasted time and effort
   B. Improving productivity
   C. Focusing on unimportant tasks
   D. Setting and achieving long-term goals

3. What should you do to develop a personal sense of time?

   A. Rely on your memory to track time
   B. Examine how you managed past time objectively
   C. Avoid analyzing how you spend your time
   D. Depend on others to manage your time

4. Identifying long-term goals involves focusing on which key areas of life?

   A. Wealth, Fame, Relationships, Health
   B. Self and Well-being, Community and Humanity, Home and Family, Business and Career
   C. Travel, Leisure, Education, Social Media
   D. None of the above

5. Why is weekly planning recommended over daily planning?

   A. It is easier and less time-consuming
   B. It focuses on urgent tasks only
   C. It eliminates the need for monthly goals
   D. It helps to take better control of your life

6. What percentage of your time produces the majority of your high-quality output?

   A. 50% B. 20% C. 80% D. 30%

7. What is 'committed time'?

   A. Time that is wasted and cannot be recovered
   B. Time that you can choose to spend as you wish
   C. Time that is scheduled and fully occupied
   D. Time spent on leisure activities

8. Which of the following is NOT a part of managing your health?

   A. Getting enough sleep
   B. Exercising regularly
   C. Avoiding holidays
   D. Applying moderation to diet

9. What is a common reason people struggle with time management?

   A. They don't have enough tasks to fill their time
   B. They fail to prioritize effectively
   C. They always plan weekly
   D. They focus on long-term goals only

10. What should you focus on to achieve high returns in your activities?

    A. Completing all tasks, regardless of importance
    B. Identifying and concentrating on high-return activities
    C. Avoiding planning and scheduling
    D. Spending more time on leisure activities

1. B	2. C	3. B	4. B	5. D	6. B	7. B	8. C	9. B	10. B

5.10 SOCIAL SKILLS

11. What is social etiquette?

    A. How to behave in a bathroom
    B. How to behave at work
    C. How to behave in society
    D. How to behave during a wedding

12. Which of the following is a bathroom etiquette?

    A. Leave the restroom untidy
    B. Leave the restroom clean and tidy
    C. Talk loudly in the restroom
    D. Use any available restroom

13. Which type of etiquette refers to behavior at work?

    A. Social etiquette
    B. Corporate etiquette
    C. Wedding etiquette
    D. Eating etiquette

14. Which of the following best suits for wedding etiquette?

    A. Arriving late
    B. Drinking uncontrollably
    C. Behaving sensibly
    D. Peeping into others' cubicles

15. Which is a meeting etiquette?

    A. Food and drinks
    B. A notepad and pen
    C. Your favourite book
    D. A laptop for personal use

16. How should you handle telephone etiquette?

    A. Put the other person on long holds
    B. Speak without greeting the other person
    C. Take care of your pitch and tone
    D. Ignore the caller

17. An important part of eating etiquette is?

    A. Making noise while eating
    B. Not making noise while eating
    C. Leaving the table early
    D. Ignoring others at the table

18. Why etiquettes are important?

    A. It makes you a cultured individual
    B. It enables you to speak loudly
    C. It allows you to ignore others
    D. It helps you avoid responsibilities

19. Identify the key way to improve social skills?

    A. Pretending to be someone else
    B. Being responsible for your actions
    C. Ignoring other people's feelings
    D. Being loud and outgoing

20. Why attentiveness is important in a social interaction?

    A. It shows you are uninterested
    B. It helps you dominate the conversation
    C. It helps in effective conversation and interaction
    D. It allows you to interrupt frequently

1. C	2. B	3. B	4. C	5. B	6. C	7. B	8. A	9. B	10. C

5.11 IMPORTANCE OF GROUP/TEAM WORK

1. Define a group?

   A. One person working alone
   B. Two or more people interacting to achieve a common objective
   C. People who never communicate
   D. A group of people who dislike each other

2. What is a Friendship Group?

   A. A group formed to accomplish work goals
   B. A group that meets members' personal security and belonging needs
   C. A group created by the management
   D. A group that meets online only

3. Which group is created by management to accomplish certain goals?

   A. Friendship Group
   B. Informal Group
   C. Task Group
   D. Social Group

4. Characteristic feature of an effective group is?

   A. Members do not communicate freely
   B. Members have no shared goals
   C. Members support agreed-upon guidelines and procedures
   D. Members work alone

5. Why group work is important?

   A. It allows people to work alone
   B. It utilizes resources to reach pre-determined goals and targets
   C. It avoids achieving common objectives
   D. It does not require communication

6. Which one of the following is an example of group work?

   A. An individual writing a book alone
   B. India achieving freedom in 1947
   C. A single person managing a company
   D. People living in complete isolation

7. What is a team? Or Define team?

   A. Two or more people who are interdependent and share responsibility for outcomes
   B. Individuals working separately
   C. People who never meet
   D. A single person doing all the work

8. Which type of team focuses on specific issues and develops potential solutions?

   A. Functional Teams
   B. Problem Solving Teams
   C. Cross-Functional Teams
   D. Social Teams

9. The key aim of teamwork is________.

   A. Working alone
   B. Avoiding collaboration

C. Ignoring team members' strengths
D. Group synergy and achieving high quality through combined contributions

10. Why cooperation and respect is important in group/ team work?

A. It leads to achieving a shared task or goal together
B. It allows individuals to work alone
C. It avoids making decisions
D. It reduces the need for communication

1. B	2. B	3. C	4. C	5. B	6. B	7. A	8. B	9. D	10. A

5.12 CAREER COUNSELLING

1. What is career counselling?

A. A method of teaching
B. A type of physical training
C. A form of entertainment
D. Counselling on issues related to an individual's career

2. Who can benefit from career counselling?

A. Only seniors
B. Only graduates
C. Freshmen, sophomores, juniors, seniors, and alumni
D. Only professionals

3. What degree does a career counsellor typically hold?

A. Bachelor's degree
B. Master's degree
C. Doctorate degree
D. Associate degree

4. Identify one of the key benefits of career counselling?

   A. Learning a new language
   B. Physical fitness improvement
   C. Determining a student's true potential
   D. Travel opportunities

5. What is the main focus of career counselling?

   A. Deciding what sports to play
   B. Knowing and understanding oneself and the world of work
   C. Learning cooking skills
   D. Improving artistic skills

1. D	2. C	3. B	4. C	5. B

5.13 SSB PROCEDURE

1. How many stages are there in the SSB procedure?

   A. One B. Two C. Three D. Four

2. The first day of SSB procedure is called as________.

   A. Conference Day
   B. Testing Day
   C. Interview Day
   D. Reporting Day

3. What does PPDT stand for?

   A. Physical Preparation and Development Training
   B. Personal Performance and Development Training
   C. Professional Preparation and Development Test
   D. Picture Perception and Discussion Test

4. What is the main purpose of the GTO tasks?

   A. To test physical strength
   B. To evaluate academic knowledge
   C. To judge qualities during group performance
   D. To check artistic abilities

5. What does TAT in psychological testing stand for?

   A. Task Analysis Test
   B. Thematic Appreciation Test
   C. Technical Aptitude Test
   D. Thematic Apperception Test

6. What is the purpose of the final group task (FGT) in the SSB procedure?

   A. To assess physical endurance
   B. To provide another chance to show your potential
   C. To test artistic skills
   D. To evaluate cooking skills

1. B	2. D	3. D	4. C	5. D	6. B

5.14 INTERVIEW SKILLS

1. What is the other name for a CV?

   A. Biography
   B. Resume
   C. Letter of inten
   D. Self-appraisal

2. What should you do before attending an interview?

   A. Ignore research
   B. Do your homework about the company or college
   C. Forget to prepare questions
   D. Arrive late

3. What should you bring to an interview?

   A. Extra copies of your resume
   B. A photo album
   C. Your favourite book
   D. Sports equipment

4. How should men dress for an interview?

   A. Jeans and a t-shirt
   B. Pants, collared shirt, tie, sports coat, and shoes
   C. Shorts and sneakers
   D. Casual wear

5. What should you avoid during an interview?

   A. Paying attention to the interviewer
   B. Displaying knowledge of the subject
   C. Answering honestly
   D. Arguing if you disagree with the interviewer

6. How should you respond if you don't know the answer to a question?

   A. Make up an answer
   B. Respond honestly that you don't know much about that topic
   C. Ignore the question
   D. Change the subject

7. What should you do at the end of an interview?

   A. Leave immediately without saying anything
   B. Express your gratitude for the opportunity
   C. Argue about your qualifications
   D. Hand out business cards

8. What is the most important thing to display during an interview?

   A. Nervous mannerisms
   B. Disinterest
   C. Enthusiasm and high interest for the job
   D. Ignorance

1. B	2. B	3. A	4. B	5. D	6. B	7. B	8. C

06

Leadership

6.1 IMPORTANT LEADERSHIP TRAITS

1. Which of the following is NOT a leadership trait?

   A. Alertness
   B. Bearing
   C. Aggressiveness
   D. Integrity

2. Courage in leadership is described as

   A. Physical strength and stamina
   B. Mental state strengthened by spiritual and intellectual sources
   C. The ability to dominate others
   D. The power to make decisions quickly

3. Which leadership trait involves a leader making prompt decisions and clearly announcing?

   A. Initiative
   B. Decisiveness
   C. Judgment
   D. Enthusiasm

4. Dependability in leadership requires ________

   A. Being physically strong
   B. Prioritizing personal conveniences
   C. Reliability and setting high standards
   D. Avoiding difficult tasks

5. What is the significance of endurance in leadership?

   A. It helps inspire the team to produce extra endurance needed to win
   B. It ensures a leader can fight the longest battles alone.
   C. It allows leaders to delegate tasks effectively
   D. It is necessary for physical appearance

6. Which leadership trait is associated with handling unpleasant tasks without complaining?

   A. Unselfishness
   B. Dependability
   C. Enthusiasm
   D. Endurance

7. A leader who is approachable and easy to talk to demonstrates which trait?

   A. Tact
   B. Knowledge
   C. Justice
   D. Bearing

8. What denotes desirable physical appearance, dress, and deportment?

   A. Alertness
   B. Bearing
   C. Courage
   D. Decisiveness

9. What helps a leader to pick up fleeting opportunities at the right time?

   A. Courage
   B. Decisiveness
   C. Alertness
   D. Endurance

10. What is the ability to remain unperturbed in a crisis and make decisions promptly?

    A. Decisiveness
    B. Initiative
    C. Knowledge
    D. Enthusiasm

11. What quality is essential for solving a problem or making a plan?

    A. Endurance
    B. Decisiveness
    C. Integrity
    D. Judgment

12. Which of the following is NOT an indicator of leadership effectiveness?

    A. Morale
    B. Team Spirit
    C. Wealth
    D. Competence

13. What does mental and physical endurance in a leader inspire?

    A. More personal convenience
    B. Routine task completion
    C. Extra endurance required to win
    D. Emotional courage

14. Leaders who demonstrate enthusiasm:

    A. Show a lack of emotion
    B. Avoid taking risks
    C. Focus solely on their own tasks
    D. Inspire and motivate their team

15. What does initiative in leadership involve?

    A. Taking proactive steps to address issues
    B. Waiting for others to make decisions
    C. Delegating all tasks
    D. Avoiding responsibility

16. A leader demonstrating tact will:

    A. Be insensitive to others' feelings
    B. Communicate with sensitivity and respect

C. Avoid difficult conversations
D. Prioritize their own opinions

17. Personal growth in leadership can be achieved by:

    A. Avoiding feedback from others
    B. Seeking continuous learning and self-improvement
    C. Sticking to familiar methods
    D. Focusing solely on strengths

18. Which trait is essential for effective problem-solving in leadership?

    A. Patience
    B. Impulsiveness
    C. Stubbornness
    D. Passivity

19. A leader's ability to adapt to change demonstrates:

    A. Flexibility
    B. Rigidity
    C. Indifference
    D. Neglect

20. Effective communication in leadership includes ________

    A. Listening actively and providing clear instructions
    B. Dominating conversations
    C. Avoiding feedback
    D. Focusing only on verbal communication

21. What is a key component of active listening?

    A. Interrupting frequently
    B. Giving full attention to the speaker
    C. Planning a response while the other person is speaking
    D. Dismissing the speaker's concerns

22. Clarity in communication helps to________.

    A. Create confusion among team members
    B. Ensure that everyone understands their roles and responsibilities
    C. Avoid addressing team issues
    D. Focus on individual achievements

23. Effective decision-making requires ________.

    A. Rushing to conclusions
    B. Ignoring team input
    C. Making arbitrary choices
    D. Considering all relevant information and potential outcomes

24. What is an essential aspect of collaborative decision-making?

    A. Overruling team input
    B. Making decisions independently
    C. Encouraging team members to contribute ideas and feedback
    D. Avoiding discussions

25. A good leader balances.

    A. Personal interests and team goals
    B. Conflict and harmony
    C. Rigidity and adaptability
    D. Authority and collaboration

26. Transparency in leadership helps to ________

    A. Hide important information
    B. Confuse team members

C. Build trust and credibility
D. Focus on individual success

27. What quality is described as "display of genuine interest and zeal"?

A. Integrity
B. Enthusiasm
C. Judgment
D. Dependability

28. What trait involves the willingness to act without orders?

A. Initiative
B. Endurance
C. Decisiveness
D. Knowledge

29. What must a leader always be with themselves and their team?

A. Self-serving
B. Honest and show integrity
C. Dishonest
D. Secretive

30. What quality is essential for assessing various factors and making wise decisions?

A. Enthusiasm
B. Initiative
C. Knowledge
D. Judgment

31. What does loyalty to subordinates and superiors create?

A. Stronger relationships and unity
B. Division
C. Apathy
D. Conflict

1. C	2. B	3. B	4. C	5. A	6. A	7. A	8. B	9. C	10. A
11. B	12. C	13. C	14. D	15. A	16. B	17. B	18. A	19. A	20. A
21. B	22. B	23. D	24. C	25. D	26. C	27. B	28. A	29. B	30. D
31. A									

6.2 INDICATORS OF LEADERSHIP AND EVALUATION (MORALE, TEAM SPIRIT, COMPETENCE AND DISCIPLINE)

1. Which statement best describes morale in a team setting?

   A. It is the physical strength of the team members
   B. It is the positive state of mind and confidence
   C. It is the strict adherence to rules and regulations
   D. It is the financial status of the team

2. Factors for evaluating team spirit includes ________

   A. The individual wealth of team members
   B. Expressions of enthusiasm and participation in activities
   C. The strict discipline enforced by the leader
   D. The physical fitness of team members

3. What is essential for maintaining discipline within a team?

   A. High level of personal convenience
   B. Quick and willing obedience to instructions
   C. Strong competitiveness
   D. Frequent rewards

4. How competence in a team is shown?

   A. Physical appearance and fitness of members
   B. The financial status of team members
   C. The length of time the team has been together
   D. The individual preferences of team members

5. Team spirit in a group can be evaluated by

   A. The amount of discipline enforced
   B. The personal achievements of the leader
   C. Expressions of individual enthusiasm
   D. The financial success of the team

6. How team spirit can be fostered?

   A. Promoting collective efforts and collaboration
   B. Encouraging individual achievements over group goals
   C. Reducing communication among team members
   D. Increasing individual rewards

7. To build team spirit, a leader should do________.

   A. Encourage competition among team members
   B. Foster a sense of belonging and unity
   C. Focus on individual tasks
   D. Reduce collaborative efforts

8. Strong relationships within a team are built on ________.

   A. Distrust and secrecy
   B. Individualism
   C. Frequent conflicts
   D. Mutual respect and open communication

9. A leader can strengthen team relationships by________.

   A. Ignoring team members' concerns
   B. Promoting teamwork and collaboration
   C. Prioritizing personal goals
   D. Reducing team interactions

10. How a leader handles failures?

   A. Ignoring it
   B. Analyzing the reasons for failure and learning from it
   C. Blaming others
   D. Giving up easily

11. What is a productive response to failure?

   A. Avoiding risk-taking
   B. Punishing the team
   C. Denying responsibility
   D. Using failure as a learning opportunity

12. What is an effective mentorship?

   A. Guiding and supporting mentees in their development
   B. Dictating actions
   C. Ignoring mentees' goals
   D. Focusing solely on one's own career

13. What do you mean by a mentor?

   A. Provide constructive feedback and encouragement
   B. Avoid giving feedback
   C. Focus on criticizing mistakes
   D. Overlook achievements

14. Conflict resolution in a team requires ________.

    A. Ignoring the issue
    B. Blaming individuals
    C. Addressing the conflict promptly and fairly
    D. Avoiding discussions

15. Which of the following is a key strategy in conflict resolution?

    A. Encourage open communication and understanding
    B. Escalate the conflict
    C. Focus on winning the argument
    D. Avoid addressing the issue

16. What role does empathy play in conflict resolution?

    A. It creates more conflict
    B. It helps to understand different perspectives and find common ground
    C. It is irrelevant
    D. It encourages dominance

17. How trust in a team is built?

    A. Being consistent and reliable
    B. Avoiding team interaction
    C. Frequently changing decisions
    D. Keeping secrets

18. What is an outcome of trust within a team?

    A. Increased conflict
    B. Decreased morale
    C. Enhanced collaboration and productivity
    D. Greater individualism

19. A leader inspires their team by ________.

    A. Setting an example through his actions and attitude
    B. Avoiding interaction
    C. Focusing solely on tasks
    D. Promoting competition

20. What is a key factor in motivating team members?

    A. Ignoring their achievements
    B. Recognizing and rewarding their contributions
    C. Providing minimal feedback
    D. Emphasizing individual efforts over team success

21. Effective stress management for a leader is

    A. Ignoring stressors
    B. Practicing self-care and encouraging a balanced workload
    C. Increasing workload without consideration
    D. Focusing only on team issues

22. What technique can help in managing stress?

    A. Avoiding all responsibilities
    B. Overcommitting to tasks
    C. Time management and prioritization
    D. Ignoring deadlines

23. What is a goal setting in leadership?

    A. Vague and unmeasurable
    B. Specific, measurable, attainable, relevant, and time-bound (SMART)
    C. Focused on individual success only
    D. Avoided to reduce pressure

24. An example of a measurable goal is ________.

    A. Improve communication
    B. Enhance team spirit
    C. Be a better leader
    D. Increase sales by 10% in the next quarter

25. Which component is critical in achieving goals?

    A. Lack of planning
    B. Ignoring feedback
    C. Regular monitoring and adjustment
    D. Focusing on multiple goals at once

26. Which one of the following is an unethical behavior in leadership?

    A. Misusing company resources for personal benefit
    B. Transparency in decision-making
    C. Encouraging team collaboration
    D. Providing constructive feedback

27. A leader can promote team development by________.

    A. Focusing on individual achievements
    B. Providing opportunities for skill enhancement and growth
    C. Reducing team interactions
    D. Avoiding training programs

28. What is an effective team development?

    A. Ignoring team conflicts
    B. Encouraging open communication and feedback
    C. Prioritizing individual tasks
    D. Avoiding team activities

29. Innovation in a team is fostered by ________

    A. Discouraging new ideas
    B. Focusing solely on established methods
    C. Avoiding risks
    D. Encouraging creative thinking and experimentation

30. ________ is the way a leader can encourage creativity.

    A. Penalizing mistakes
    B. Providing a supportive environment for brainstorming
    C. Limiting team discussions
    D. Enforcing strict adherence to rules

31. What is empowerment in leadership?

    A. Delegating responsibilities without support
    B. Providing team members with the authority and resources to make decisions
    C. Micromanaging every task
    D. Avoiding delegation

32. What is the effect of empowering team members?

    A. Reduced motivation
    B. Decreased productivity
    C. Increased ownership and accountability
    D. Greater dependence on the leader

33. What does "bearing" in leadership entail?

    A. Ignoring personal problems
    B. Adapting to any situation regardless of its nature

C. Showing dignity and composure under all conditions
D. Being assertive and aggressive

34. An effective leader ensures discipline by________.

A. Setting clear expectations and leading by example
B. Being overly strict and unapproachable
C. Allowing team members to set their own rules
D. Ignoring disciplinary issues

35. What is competence?

A. Only a physical ability
B. An emotional state
C. Technique, tactics, and physical ability
D. Leadership by personal example

36. What is one factor considered in evaluating competence in a group?

A. Personal appearance and physical fitness
B. Devotion to duty
C. Harmonious relations
D. Attention to instructions

37. What should be the practice in relation to all instructions and plans of superiors?

A. Ignoring them
B. Questioning them frequently
C. Delaying them
D. Carrying them out to the best ability and on time

38. Which of the following best describes competence in a team?

    A. Members' ability to follow orders without question
    B. Members' effectiveness and efficiency in their duties
    C. Members' social status and background
    D. Members' adherence to strict rules

39. Emotional intelligence in leadership involves:

    A. Ignoring team members' feelings
    B. Focusing only on tasks
    C. Recognizing and managing one's own emotions and those of others
    D. Avoiding emotional interactions

40. A leader with high emotional intelligence:

    A. Understands and addresses team members' emotional needs
    B. Ignores team dynamics
    C. Prioritizes tasks over relationships
    D. Avoids conflict resolution

41. Effective delegation involves________.

    A. Retaining all responsibilities
    B. Assigning tasks based on team members' strengths and providing necessary support
    C. Avoiding task assignments
    D. Delegating without clear instructions

42. A common mistake in delegation is________.

    A. Providing clear guidance
    B. Micromanaging tasks after delegation
    C. Encouraging autonomy
    D. Offering support

43. What is cultural awareness in leadership means?

    A. Ignoring cultural differences
    B. Understanding and respecting diverse backgrounds and perspectives
    C. Enforcing a single cultural viewpoint
    D. Avoiding cultural discussions

44. A culturally aware leader will________.

    A. Promote inclusivity and celebrate diversity
    B. Discourage cultural expression
    C. Focus solely on their own culture
    D. Avoid multicultural teams

45. Effective time management for a leader involves______.

    A. Procrastinating on important tasks
    B. Taking on too many tasks at once
    C. Ignoring time constraints
    D. Prioritizing tasks and setting clear deadlines

46. A common time management mistake is________.

    A. Setting realistic goals
    B. Delegating tasks
    C. Using a planner
    D. Overcommitting to tasks and responsibilities

47. A leader with a clear vision progresses by________.

    A. Inspires and guides the team towards long-term goals
    B. Focuses on short-term gains
    C. Avoids setting goals
    D. Prioritizes immediate tasks only

48. What is strategic planning?

    A. Ignoring future trends
    B. Analyzing current conditions and forecasting future scenarios
    C. Focusing solely on present issues
    D. Avoiding long-term thinking

49. An adaptable leader is________.

    A. Resists change
    B. Welcomes and manages change effectively
    C. Sticks to old methods
    D. Avoids new challenges

50. Why an adaptability is essential?

    A. It allows leaders to remain rigid
    B. It helps leaders to respond effectively to evolving situations
    C. It discourages innovation
    D. It promotes consistency in all situations

51. When facing an ethical dilemma, a leader should ________.

    A. Prioritize personal gain
    B. Ignore ethical considerations
    C. Make a decision based on convenience

D. Consider the ethical implications and consult with others if necessary

52. Which of the following way a leader's response to unethical behavior?

A. To overlook it
B. To condone it if it benefits the team
C. To avoid getting involved
D. To address it immediately and uphold ethical standards

53. A positive work environment is characterized by ________.

A. High stress and competition
B. Mutual respect, support, and collaboration
C. Frequent conflicts
D. Lack of communication

54. How a leader can create a positive environment?

A. Fostering negativity
B. Promoting isolation
C. Encouraging teamwork and recognizing achievements
D. Ignoring team morale

1. B	2. B	3. B	4. A	5. C	6. A	7. B	8. D	9. B	10. B
11. D	12. A	13. A	14. C	15. A	16. B	17. A	18. C	19. A	20. B
21. B	22. C	23. B	24. D	25. C	26. A	27. B	28. B	29. D	30. B
31. B	32. C	33. C	34. A	35. C	36. A	37. D	38. B	39. C	40. A
41. B	42. B	43. B	44. A	45. D	46. D	47. A	48. B	49. B	50. B
51. D	52. D	53. B	54. C						

6.3 MOTIVATION AND FACTORS WHICH MOTIVATE

1. What is motivation?

   A. A material resource
   B. A spiritual factor
   C. The commitment and urge within a member to accomplish a task
   D. An intellectual factor

2. Spiritual factors in motivation help to ________

   A. Offer the highest inspiration and sustain individuals
   B. Provide physical resources
   C. Encourage intellectual discussions
   D. Increase financial wealth

3. Which of the following is a material factor that motivates people?

   A. Leadership by personal example
   B. Pride in the group
   C. Good quality resources
   D. Spiritual inspiration

4. What intellectual factor makes an individual proud of his/her group?

   A. Spirituality
   B. History of the group
   C. Material resources
   D. Leadership by personal example

5. What is a spiritual factor that can sustain a person when all hope is lost?

   A. Intellectual pride
   B. Group identity
   C. Material resources
   D. Personal example

6. Which ancient philosopher's advice is cited as a spiritual inspiration?

   A. Socrates B. Aristotle C. Krishna D. Plato

7. Which factor is NOT considered as motivational factor for individuals?

   A. Material Factors
   B. Intellectual Factors
   C. Spiritual Factors
   D. Financial Wealth

8. Material factors in motivation includes?

   A. Personal satisfaction and recognition
   B. Resources needed to improve the quality of life and goals
   C. Personal beliefs and spirituality
   D. Team spirit and loyalty

9. Leadership by personal example is a part of ________

   A. Material Factors
   B. Intellectual Factors
   C. Spiritual Factors
   D. Financial Factors

10. Intellectual factors in motivation include________

   A. Encouraging physical exercise
   B. Providing mental challenges and opportunities for growth
   C. Focusing solely on material wealth
   D. Reducing team interactions

11. What is a key aspect of spiritual factors in leadership?

    A. Providing financial incentives
    B. Implementing strict rules
    C. Encouraging a sense of purpose and meaning
    D. Offering physical rewards

1. C	2. A	3. C	4. D	5. B	6. C	7. D	8. B	9. B	10. B	11. C

6.4 MORAL VALUES AND CHARACTER TRAITS

1. What defines morale in a leadership?

    A. Loyalty to the leader
    B. Competitiveness among team members
    C. Strict adherence to rules
    D. Positive state of mind and confidence

2. Morale is often measured by:

    A. The number of hours worked
    B. The amount of money spent on the team
    C. The enthusiasm and willingness to perform
    D. The level of competition within the team

3. Which of the following actions helps improve team morale?

    A. Recognizing and celebrating team achievements
    B. Reducing team communication
    C. Prioritizing individual success
    D. Ignoring team conflicts

4. Leaders with self-control:

    A. Allow their emotions to dictate their actions
    B. Manage their reactions and maintain composure

C. Focus on their personal convenience
D. Avoid taking responsibility

5. Justice in leadership is best described as __________

A. Favoring certain team members
B. Being fair and impartial in decision-making
C. Making arbitrary decisions
D. Ignoring team conflicts

6. As per Plato, what does prudence mean?

A. Making the right decision
B. Subordinating emotions
C. Courage to stay the course
D. Giving everyone their due

7. What virtue involves staying the course and resisting temptation?

A. Prudence
B. Courage
C. Self-control
D. Justice

8. What does self-control involve?

A. Making the right decision
B. Giving everyone their due
C. Courageously enduring challenges
D. Subordinating passions and emotions

9. What does justice entail in moral values?

A. Giving every individual their due
B. Staying the course
C. Making right decisions
D. Subordinating emotions

10. What is the definition of character?

    A. A reflection of virtues and weaknesses
    B. Temporary gain leading to long-term pain
    C. A bundle of habits and behavior
    D. An inborn quality

11. What type of courage involves staking career happiness on one's judgment?

    A. Physical courage
    B. Moral courage
    C. Mental courage
    D. Intellectual courage

12. Character traits include all EXCEPT?

    A. Speaking truth
    B. Keeping one's word
    C. Seeking cheap popularity
    D. Owning up to mistakes

13. What should a person of character do when they make a mistake?

    A. Hide the mistake
    B. Ignore it
    C. Blame others
    D. Admit the mistake

14. Which character trait involves admitting and correcting one's mistakes?

    A. Courage
    B. Loyalty
    C. Honesty
    D. Humility

15. What is the consequence of speaking a lie?

    A. It gains respect
    B. It has enormous and irreversible consequences
    C. It can be taken back easily
    D. It improves one's character

16. Why self-control is important in leadership?

    A. It helps to manage passions and emotions effectively
    B. It allows for the avoidance of difficult tasks
    C. It ensures financial success
    D. It enables one to seek personal convenience

17. Personal integrity for a leader involves:

    A. Compromising values for personal gain
    B. Consistently acting in accordance with ethical principles
    C. Ignoring ethical dilemmas
    D. Being inconsistent in actions and decisions

18. Why personal integrity is crucial in leadership?

    A. It allows leaders to manipulate others
    B. It establishes trust and sets a standard for the team
    C. It focuses solely on personal success
    D. It avoids accountability

19. Self-reflection helps a leader to:

    A. Ignore personal growth
    B. Understand their strengths and areas for improvement
    C. Focus solely on external feedback
    D. Avoid personal accountability

20. A leader should engage in self-reflection:

    A. Only during crises
    B. Rarely to avoid self-criticism
    C. Regularly to ensure continuous improvement
    D. When prompted by others

21. What is the rule regarding “Business before self”?

    A. Should be avoided
    B. Should be the consistent practice
    C. Only when convenient
    D. Optional depending on situation

22. Why is integrity important in leadership?

    A. It builds trust and sets a positive example
    B. It allows leaders to manipulate others
    C. It focuses solely on personal success
    D. It avoids accountability

23. Integrity in leadership involves:

    A. Compromising personal values for convenience
    B. Upholding ethical standards consistently
    C. Prioritizing personal gain over team success
    D. Avoiding responsibility

24. What is essential for a leader to maintain integrity?

    A. Compromising values for quick gains
    B. Aligning actions with ethical standards and personal values
    C. Seeking approval from subordinates
    D. Delegating all responsibilities

25. What is an ethical leadership?

    A. Compromising values for success
    B. Seeking personal gain
    C. Avoiding responsibility
    D. Upholding moral principles consistently

1. D	2. C	3. A	4. B	5. B	6. A	7. B	8. D	9. A	10. A
11. B	12. C	13. D	14. C	15. B	16. A	17. B	18. B	19. B	20. C
21. B	22. A	23. B	24. B	25. D					

6.5 HONOUR CODE

1. According to the honour code, what should one always do?

   A. Speak truth
   B. Avoid responsibility
   C. Seek popularity
   D. Be dishonest

2. What should one do after making a mistake?

   A. Hide it
   B. Blame others
   C. Admit it
   D. Ignore it

3. What does the honour code say about cheap popularity?

   A. It is desirable
   B. It is always appreciated
   C. It should be sought after
   D. It should be avoided

4. What quality should one set an example of?

   A. Dishonesty
   B. Self-discipline
   C. Irresponsibility
   D. Favoritism

5. The Honour Code requires individuals **NOT** to __________

   A. Lie, steal, or cheat
   B. Accept responsibility for their actions
   C. Stand up for what is right
   D. Seek personal gain

6. What is a key tenet of the Honour Code?

   A. To seek personal fame
   B. To give priority to group interest over personal interest
   C. To focus on financial success
   D. To ignore team issues

7. The Honour Code emphasizes_________?

   A. Upholding truth and integrity
   B. Prioritizing personal interests
   C. Seeking personal recognition
   D. Ignoring group interests

8. Living by the Honour Code requires _________

   A. Compromising ethical values
   B. Focusing on material wealth
   C. Being a good example to others
   D. Avoiding responsibility

9. Which is a violation of the Honour Code?

   A. Admitting mistakes
   B. Being loyal to the team
   C. Standing up for what is right
   D. Lying to protect oneself

1. A	2. C	3. D	4. B	5. D	6. B	7. A	8. C	9. D

07

Disaster Management

1. Who is the head of State Disaster Management Authority (SDMA)?

   A. Chief Secretary
   B. Prime Minister
   C. Chief Minister
   D. Home Minister

2. NDMA stands for?

   A. National Disaster Mitigation Authority
   B. National Disaster Management Authority
   C. National Disaster Maintenance Authority
   D. National Disaster Monitoring Authority

3. Which organization in India is tasked with the coordination of response during a disaster?

   A. SDMA
   B. NEC
   C. DDMA
   D. NDRF

4. Who heads the National Disaster Management Authority (NDMA)?

   A. Chief Minister
   B. Prime Minister
   C. Home Minister
   D. President

5. Who has the power to constitute the National Executive Committee (NEC)?

   A. Prime Minister
   B. Home Minister
   C. Chief Minister
   D. District Collector

6. The general superintendence, direction, and control of the NDRF is done by________.

   A. State Government
   B. Central Government
   C. NDMA
   D. DDMA

7. Who heads the District Disaster Management Authority (DDMA)?

   A. Chief Minister
   B. District Collector or Deputy Commissioner
   C. Home Minister
   D. Prime Minister

8. What is the role of the National Executive Committee (NEC)?

   A. To enact disaster management laws
   B. To assist NDMA in discharge of its functions
   C. To fund disaster relief efforts
   D. To manage local disasters

9. Which type of disasters are managed by the NDRF?

   A. Natural only
   B. Man-made only
   C. Both natural and man-made
   D. Neither natural nor man-made

10. Which is NOT a natural disaster?

    A. Earthquakes
    B. Floods
    C. Terrorist attacks
    D. Cyclones

11. Which of the following is a man-made disaster?

    A. Tsunami
    B. Cyclone
    C. Industrial mishaps
    D. Avalanche

12. The term 'CBRN emergencies' stand for________.

    A. Chemical, Biological, Radiological, and Nuclear
    B. Civil, Biological, Radiological, and Nuclear
    C. Chemical, Biochemical, Radiological, and Nuclear
    D. Chemical, Biological, Radioactive, and Nuclear

13. Which body is responsible for district level disaster management?

    A. SDMA B. NDMA C. DDMA D. NEC

14. How many battalions are there in NDRF currently?

    A. Ten B. Twelve C. Fifteen D. Twenty

15. The State Disaster Management Authority (SDMA) is assisted by________.

    A. DDMA B. SDMA C. NEC D. SEC

16. Which of the following is a wind-related natural disaster?

    A. Earthquake
    B. Tsunami
    C. Cyclone
    D. Landslide

17. Which authority is responsible for monitoring, approving and implementation of the State Plan for Disaster Management?

    A. NEC B. SDMA C. DDMA D. NDMA

18. Which natural disaster is NOT caused by wind?

    A. Tornado B. Blizzards C. Floods D. Storms

19. What type of disaster is caused by contamination/ poisoning?

   A. Natural
   B. Man-made
   C. Both
   D. None

20. Who is the Co-Chairperson of the DDMA?

   A. Chief Minister
   B. Local elected representative
   C. Chief Secretary
   D. Home Minister

21. Which disaster is categorized under industrial mishaps?

   A. Earthquake
   B. Gas leaks
   C. Avalanche
   D. Cyclone

22. Who coordinates the implementation of the State Plan for Disaster Management?

   A. NDMA
   B. SDMA
   C. NEC
   D. SEC

23. Which of the following is a water-related natural disaster?

   A. Blizzards
   B. Landslides
   C. Floods
   D. Earthquakes

24. Which body is responsible for capacity building of local authorities for managing disasters?

   A. NDMA
   B. SDMA
   C. DDMAs
   D. Local Authorities

25. What percentage of the Indian landmass is prone to earthquakes?

A. 58.6% B. 40% C. 68% D. 12%

26. Which of the following is NOT a component of essential services during disasters?

A. Postal services
B. Transport services
C. Recreational services
D. Medical services

27. The NDRF units maintain close liaison with ________ during a disaster?

A. Local police
B. State Governments
C. Central Government
D. Local authorities

28. What is the function of National Disaster Response Force (NDRF)?

A. To fund disaster relief efforts
B. To assist in evacuation during disasters
C. To provide specialized response to disaster situations
D. To create disaster management policies

29. What is the purpose of the National Disaster Management Authority (NDMA)?

A. To create disaster management laws
B. To implement state disaster plans
C. To lay down policies for disaster management
D. To coordinate district-level disaster management

30. Which body prepares the National Plan for Disaster Management?

    A. NDMA B. NEC C. SDMA D. DDMA

31. The full form of SEC is________.

    A. State Emergency Committee
    B. State Executive Committee
    C. State Evacuation Committee
    D. State Environmental Committee

32. Which natural disaster is caused by the movement of tectonic plates?

    A. Cyclone
    B. Tsunami
    C. Avalanche
    D. Earthquake

33. Which one of the following is NOT a function of the State Executive Committee (SEC)?

    A. Coordinate the implementation of the National Policy
    B. Recommend provision of funds for mitigation
    C. Review the developmental plans of different departments
    D. Monitor the implementation of the National Plan

34. Who does the general superintendence, direction and control of NDRF?

    A. NDMA
    B. NEC
    C. President
    D. SDMA

35. The command and control of NDRF lies with________.

    A. Chief Minister
    B. Director General of Civil Defence and NDRF

C. Prime Minister
D. District Collector

36. Which of the following is an example of a chemical disaster?

A. Earthquake
B. Flood
C. Gas leak
D. Tornado

37. Which body monitors the implementation of guidelines issued by the NDMA?

A. SDMA
B. NEC
C. SEC
D. DDMA

38. The acronym DDMA stand for________.

A. District Disaster Management Act
B. Disaster District Management Authority
C. District Disaster Management Authority
D. District Disaster Mitigation Authority

39. Which of the following is a structural measure for disaster risk reduction?

A. Public awareness campaigns
B. Emergency drills
C. Capacity building programs
D. Building codes

40. What is the primary function of the State Disaster Response Force (SDRF)?

A. To create disaster management policies
B. To assist in rescue and relief operations
C. To fund disaster relief efforts
D. To train local authorities in disaster management

41. Which natural disaster is characterized by heavy snowfall and strong winds?

A. Tsunami
B. Blizzard
C. Earthquake
D. Cyclone

42. Which of the following is a non-structural measure for disaster risk reduction?

A. Building levees
B. Constructing dams
C. Enforcing land-use planning
D. Retrofitting buildings

43. What is the role of local authorities in disaster management?

A. To implement national policies
B. To create state-level disaster plans
C. To assist in disaster preparedness and response
D. To fund disaster management projects

44. Which of the following is an example of a biological disaster?

A. Earthquake
B. Tsunami
C. Epidemic
D. Cyclone

45. Which type of disaster involves the sudden release of gases or vapors?

A. Biological disaster
B. Chemical disaster
C. Geological disaster
D. Meteorological disaster

46. Who approves the National Plan for Disaster Management?

A. NDMA
B. NEC
C.SDMA
D. Central Government

47. Which of the following is a wind-related natural disaster?

A. Earthquake
B. Flood
C. Tornado
D. Tsunami

48. Which type of natural disaster includes floods and excessive rains?

A. Wind related
B. Water related
C. Earth related
D. Fire related

49. Which of the following is an earth-related natural disaster?

A. Cyclone
B. Tsunami
C. Drought
D. Storm

50. What type of disaster is caused by gas leaks and explosions?

A. Natural
B. Fire
C. Terrorist activity
D. Industrial mishap

51. Which of the following is a man-made fire disaster?

A. Volcanic eruption
B. Forest fire in tropical countries
C. Earthquake
D. Blizzard

52. Which type of man-made disaster involves serial blasts or explosions in public areas?

    A. Industrial mishap
    B. Fire
    C. Terrorist activities
    D. Ecological

53. Pollution of air and water falls under which category of man-made disaster?

    A. Accidents
    B. Industrial mishaps
    C. Warfare
    D. Ecological

54. Which of the following is an example of warfare-related disaster?

    A. Nuclear accident
    B. Flash flood
    C. Road accident
    D. Earthquake

55. Building collapse is an example of which type of man-made disaster?

    A. Fire
    B. Industrial mishap
    C. Accidents
    D. Ecological

56. Which of the following is considered an essential service?

    A. Postal services
    B. Movie theaters
    C. Sports events
    D. Shopping malls

57. Which essential service includes rail, road, air, and sea?

    A. Medical services
    B. Transport services
    C. Production services
    D. Security services

58. NCC cadets can assist in hospitals by working as:

    A. Cooks
    B. Engineers
    C. Nurses
    D. Drivers

59. What is the role of Civil Defence Corps in disaster management?

    A. Cooking services
    B. Warden's service
    C. Entertainment services
    D. Banking services

60. NCC cadets can help in emergency situations by

    A. Building new houses
    B. Selling goods
    C. Salvaging destroyed structures
    D. Organizing sports events

61. Who organizes the action groups of NCC cadets?

    A. District authorities
    B. School teachers
    C. Hospital staff
    D. CO Unit / Group Commander

62. Which service is part of the Civil Defence Corps?

    A. Tourism Service
    B. Fire Fighting Service
    C. Entertainment Service
    D. Educational Service

1. C	2. B	3. D	4. B	5. B	6. C	7. B	8. B	9. C	10. C
11. C	12. A	13. C	14. B	15. D	16. C	17. B	18. C	19. B	20. B
21. B	22. D	23. C	24. D	25. A	26. C	27. B	28. C	29. C	30. B
31. B	32. D	33. B	34.	35. B	36. C	37. B	38. C	39. D	40. B
41. B	42. C	43. C	44. C	45. B	46. D	47. C	48. B	49. B	50. D
51. B	52. C	53. D	54. A	55. C	56. A	57. B	58. C	59. B	60. C
61. D	62. B								

7.1 FIRE SERVICES AND FIRE FIGHTING

1. What has led to an increase in fire incidents in homes?

   A. Increased standard of living
   B. Lack of cooking gas
   C. Reduced use of electrical goods
   D. Absence of air conditioners

2. Which of the following is NOT essential for the creation of fire?

   A. Oxygen
   B. Water
   C. Sufficient heat
   D. Combustible material

3. Which is necessary to raise the temperature of fuel to its burning point?

   A. Air
   B. Sufficient heat
   C. Cold
   D. Water

4. What should you check in the kitchen to prevent fire incidents?

   A. Gas cylinder and gas pipe for leakage
   B. Refrigerator temperature
   C. Water supply
   D. Oven door

5. How can you prevent electrical fires in your home?

   A. Use low-quality electrical items
   B. Overload electrical circuits
   C. Ensure electrical gadgets are switched off when not in use
   D. Keep flammable materials near electrical circuits

6. What is NOT a recommended practice to prevent fires in public places?

   A. Avoid igniting firecrackers near petrol pumps
   B. Leave burning cigarettes in public dustbins
   C. Avoid firecrackers in crowded markets
   D. Keep inflammable materials away in AC offices

7. Which method of extinguishing fire involves removing fuel or combustible material?

   A. Cooling
   B. Smothering
   C. Starvation
   D. Heating

8. What is used to lower the temperature of burning material in cooling?

   A. Sand
   B. Water
   C. Foam
   D. Oxygen

9. What is the purpose of smothering in firefighting?

   A. Increase heat
   B. Remove fuel
   C. Restrict oxygen supply
   D. Add combustible material

10. How many persons are there in a House Fire Party?

   A. Two
   B. Four
   C. Six
   D. Eight

11. What equipment does a House Fire Party NOT carry?

   A. Stirrup pump
   B. Hand axe
   C. Water bucket
   D. Fire extinguisher

12. The members of Auxiliary Fire Services usually drawn from________.

    A. Police
    B. Home Guards
    C. Fire department
    D. Medical staff

13. Which firefighting equipment is designed for use on small fires?

    A. Stirrup pumps
    B. Fire beaters
    C. Fire extinguishers
    D. Buckets

14. Which type of extinguisher is used for fires involving ordinary combustible materials?

    A. Soda acid extinguishers
    B. CTC carbon dioxide extinguishers
    C. Foam type extinguishers
    D. Dry chemical extinguishers

15. What is the primary use of foam type or dry chemical powder extinguishers?

    A. Extinguishing electrical fires
    B. Extinguishing ordinary fires
    C. Extinguishing fires involving inflammable liquids
    D. Extinguishing small fires

16. Disadvantage of fire extinguishers is________.

    A. Easy to operate
    B. Portable
    C. High cost
    D. Useful in initial stages of fire

17. What is an advantage of fire extinguishers?

    A. Requires multiple people to operate
    B. Easy to operate
    C. Difficult to maintain
    D. Limited use time

18. The water consumption of a stirrup pump/minute is?

    A. 1-2 liters
    B. 2.8 liters
    C. 3.8-5.7 liters
    D. 10 liters

19. What is the use of buckets in firefighting?

    A. Storing water and sand
    B. Producing foam
    C. Containing chemicals
    D. Pumping water

20. Which equipment is ideal for separating burning and unburnt combustible material?

    A. Stirrup pump
    B. Fire extinguisher
    C. Bucket
    D. Fire beaters and hooks

21. Which type of fire extinguisher is designed to use for extinguishing fires involving inflammable liquids like oils and fats?

    A. Soda Acid Extinguishers
    B. Foam Type or Dry Chemical Powder Extinguishers
    C. Water Extinguishers
    D. Stirrup Pumps

22. CTC Carbon dioxide and Dry Chemical Extinguishers are mainly used for which type of fires?

    A. Fires involving ordinary combustible materials
    B. Fires involving inflammable liquids
    C. Fires involving live electrical equipment
    D. Fires in open areas

23. Which of the following is NOT a category of firefighting equipment?

    A. Fire Extinguishers
    B. Stirrup Pumps
    C. Fire Alarms
    D. Buckets

24. Which category of firefighting equipment can be used to physically separate burning and unburnt materials?

    A. Fire Extinguishers
    B. Buckets
    C. Stirrup Pumps
    D. Fire Beaters and Hooks

25. What type of extinguisher is used for fires involving ordinary combustible material?

    A. Foam Type Extinguishers
    B. CTC Carbon Dioxide Extinguishers
    C. Soda Acid Extinguishers
    D. Dry Chemical Powder Extinguishers

26. Foam Type or Dry Chemical Powder Extinguishers are meant for extinguishing fires involving which substances?

    A. Wood and paper
    B. Electrical equipment
    C. Inflammable liquids like oils and fats
    D. Metal fires

27. Which fire extinguisher is mainly used to fight fires involving live electrical equipment?

    A. Soda Acid Extinguishers
    B. CTC Carbon Dioxide Extinguishers
    C. Water Extinguishers
    D. Foam Extinguishers

28. What is the purpose of Dry Chemical Powder in foam type extinguishers?

    A. Cooling effect
    B. Isolation from oxygen (air)
    C. Conducting electricity
    D. Increasing temperature

1. A	2. B	3. B	4. A	5. C	6. B	7. C	8. B	9. C	10. B
11. D	12. B	13. A	14. A	15. C	16. C	17. B	18. C	19. A	20. D
21. B	22. C	23. C	24. D	25. C	26. C	27. B	28. B		

08

Social Service and Community Development

1. What is Social Case Work?

   A. Improving productivity in rural areas
   B. Helping the individual to make maximum use of the established community
   C. Increasing employment opportunities
   D. Providing housing and rehabilitation

2. How 'Social Group Work' seek to help individuals with?

   A. By utilizing their fullest capacity for their own welfare and the group's welfare
   B. By making use of established community resources
   C. By organizing social assistance programs
   D. By developing infrastructure in rural areas

3. What is the focus of Community Organization?

   A. Providing old age support systems
   B. Helping groups of individuals work together for community welfare
   C. Offering recreational activities
   D. Improving medical care and family planning

4. Which of the following is NOT a social service activity?

   A. Education
   B. Provision of Cooking Fuel

C. Family Welfare Medical Care
D. Space Exploration

5. How can NCC cadets contribute to society?

A. By helping a blind man cross a road
B. By investing in stock markets
C. By organizing corporate events
D. By running a business

6. What is the objective of rural development?

A. To increase urbanization
B. To improve living standards by providing basic needs
C. To develop technology parks
D. To build highways

7. MGNREGA stands for________.

A. Mahatma Gandhi National Rural Employment Guarantee Act
B. Modern Government National Revenue and Expenditure Act
C. Mahatma Gandhi National Road Expansion Act
D. Modern Government National Resource Expansion Act

8. What is the aim of Pradhan Mantri Gram Sadak Yojana (PMGSY)?

A. To provide housing for the poor
B. To offer medical insurance to citizens
C. To give all-weather road connectivity to unconnected villages
D. To increase internet connectivity

9. When was the National Social Assistance Programme (NSAP) launched?

   A. 1985-86
   B. 1995-96
   C. 2005-06
   D. 2015-16

10. What is the goal of Sansad Adarsh Gram Yojana(SAGY)?

    A. To develop urban areas
    B. To construct highways
    C. To promote international trade
    D. To develop model villages through MPs' initiative

11. Which component is NOT part of Pradhan Mantri Awas Yojana (PMAY)?

    A. Urban (PMAY-U)
    B. Gramin (PMAY-G)
    C. Coastal (PMAY-C)
    D. None of the above

12. Which age group can enroll in Jeevan Jyoti Bima Yojna?

    A. 18 to 50 years
    B. 20 to 60 years
    C. 10 to 40 years
    D. 30 to 70 years

13. Which is NOT a major objective of Pradhan Mantri Krishi Sinchai Yojna (PMKSY)?

    A. Expand cultivable area under irrigation
    B. Develop space technology
    C. Improve On-farm water use efficiency
    D. Enhance recharge of aquifers

14. The Atal Pension Yojana (APY) aims to do________.

    A. Provide scholarships to students
    B. Offer fixed minimum monthly pension to workers
    C. Promote international travel
    D. Develop industrial parks

15. What is the coverage of Pradhan Mantri Suraksha Bima Yojana (PMSBY) for accidental death?

A. Rs. 50,000
B. Rs. 1 lakh
C. Rs. 2 lakh
D. Rs. 5 lakh

16. Which activity is NOT a contribution of NGOs?

A. Blood Donation
B. Tree Plantation
C. Adult Literacy
D. Developing software

17. What role does NGOs play in society?

A. Investing in real estate
B. Working towards social welfare and nation building
C. Operating multinational corporations
D. Promoting luxury goods

18. How youth can contribute to social service?

A. By working in hospitals to attend helpless patients
B. By investing in the stock market
C. By playing video games
D. By traveling abroad for leisure

19. Identify the program that can be organized by NCC cadets to promote awareness?

A. social issues like female foeticide and drug abuse
B. Sports tournaments
C. Business seminars
D. Fashion shows

20. Which is NOT a feature of Pradhan Mantri Jeevan Jyoti Yojana (PMJJBY)?

    A. Available to persons in the age group of 18 to 50 years
    B. Annual life insurance coverage in case of death
    C. Risk coverage of Rs. 2 lakhs in case of death
    D. Only available to government employees

1. B	2. A	3. B	4. D	5. A	6. B	7. A	8. C	9. B	10. D
11. C	12. A	13. B	14. B	15. C	16. D	17. B	18. A	19. A	20. D

8.1 SWACHH BHARAT ABHIYAN

1. What is the primary objective of the Swachh Bharat Abhiyan?

   A. To beautify urban areas
   B. To reduce or eliminate open defecation
   C. To promote tourism
   D. To build new infrastructure

2. When was the Swachh Bharat Abhiyan officially launched?

   A. 15 August 2014
   B. 26 January 2014
   C. 02 October 2014
   D. 14 November 2014

3. Who launched the Swachh Bharat Abhiyan?

   A. Dr. Manmohan Singh
   B. Narendra Modi
   C. Pranab Mukherjee
   D. Amit Shah

4. How many statutory cities and towns are targeted under the Swachh Bharat Abhiyan?

   A. 1024 B. 2041 C. 3041 D. 4041

5. What is the projected cost for achieving an Open-Defecation Free (ODF) India by 2 October 2019?

   A. ₹1.96 lakh crore (US$30 billion)
   B. ₹1.50 lakh crore (US$25 billion)
   C. ₹2.50 lakh crore (US$35 billion)
   D. ₹2.00 lakh crore (US$32 billion)

6. Which organization was awarded for its outstanding contribution towards the Swachh Bharat Mission?

   A. National Service Scheme (NSS)
   B. Indian Red Cross Society
   C. Bharat Scouts and Guides
   D. National Cadet Corps (NCC)

7. What is "Sauchh Abhiyan" specifically focused on?

   A. Cleaning rivers
   B. Constructing individual sanitary latrines
   C. Promoting recycling
   D. Planting trees

8. How long did the NCC's Swachata Pakhwada campaign last?

   A. One week C. One month
   B. Two weeks D. Six months

9. Which significant target date of milestone is linked for achieving Open-Defecation Free India?

   A. 150th anniversary of the birth of Mahatma Gandhi
   B. 75th anniversary of Indian Independence
   C. 100th anniversary of Republic Day
   D. 50th anniversary of the Green Revolution

10. Which of the following is NOT a benefit of Sauchh Abhiyan?

    A. Converting dry latrines into low-cost sanitary latrines
    B. Providing facility of hand pumping
    C. Building new highways
    D. Construction of drains for disposal of solid and liquid wastes

1. B	2. C	3. B	4. D	5. A	6. D	7. B	8. B	9. A	10. C

8.2 SOCIAL SECURITY

1. What does social security aim to provide?

   A. Luxury goods
   B. Basic needs to citizens
   C. Entertainment
   D. Travel allowances

2. Who contributes to social security funding?

   A. Only the government
   B. Only employees
   C. Employees and employers
   D. Only employers

3. What percentage of the world's population has access to comprehensive social security according to the ILO 2014?

   A. 50% B. 75% C. 90% D. 27%

4. Social welfare services aim to prevent and reform what?

   A. Physical fitness
   B. Disabilities or disorganization
   C. Financial planning
   D. Real estate issues

5. Which type of social security includes retirement pensions and disability insurance?

   A. Social Insurance C. Services
   B. Basic Security D. Health Insurance

1. B	2. C	3. D	4. B	5. A

8.3 SOCIAL EVILS: FEMALE FOETICIDE

1. What is a major cause of female foeticide in India?

   A. Extreme desire to have a male child
   B. Economic prosperity
   C. Lack of technology
   D. Government policies

2. What is a common excuse used for performing abortions that lead to female foeticide?

   A. Religious beliefs C. Lack of facilities
   B. High medical costs D. Unwanted pregnancy

3. What is a significant effect of female foeticide?

   A. Increased sex ratio
   B. Higher employment rates
   C. Decreased crime rates
   D. Population drop

4. What is a proposed measure to prevent female foeticide?

   A. Encouraging male child preference
   B. High fines for illegal sex determination
   C. Reducing education incentives for girls
   D. Promoting male dominance in society

5. What is the sex ratio in India according to the 2011 census?

   A. 914 girls for 1000 boys
   B. 800 girls for 1000 boys
   C. 1000 girls for 1000 boys
   D. 700 girls for 1000 boys

1. A	2. D	3. D	4. B	5. A

8.4 SOCIAL EVILS: DOWRY

1. Which economic factor contributes to the dowry system?

   A. Bride's economic status
   B. Technological advancements
   C. Social media influence
   D. Government subsidies

2. In which part of India is the dowry system more prevalent?

A. Northern India C. Southern India
B. Western India D. Eastern India

3. Dowry in Indian Muslims is referred to as what?

A. Sadqa B. Zakat C. Fitrah D. Jahez

4. What is a recommended measure to prevent dowry?

A. Offering larger dowries
B. Educating girls to become economically independent
C. Encouraging early marriages
D. Reducing women's rights

5. Which religious texts prescribe the giving of dowry?

A. Bible B. Quran C. Vedas D. Torah

1. A	2. A	3. D	4. B	5. C

8.5 SOCIAL EVILS: CORRUPTION

1. What is a suggested measure to prevent corruption?

A. Reducing education on corruption
B. Encouraging bribes
C. Ignoring corruption cases
D. Speedy trial and exemplary punishment

2. Ensuring transparency in all dealings is aimed at preventing what?

A. Gender inequality
B. Corruption
C. Education disparities
D. Environmental pollution

3. Who should have full freedom to investigate corruption cases?

   A. The Lok Pal or Lokayukta
   B. Corporate entities
   C. The President
   D. General public

4. What role should the police play in preventing corruption?

   A. Ignoring minor cases
   B. Supporting corrupt officials
   C. Acting fearlessly against corruption
   D. Delaying trials

5. Education on corruption should target which sections of society?

   A. Only the rich
   B. Only government officials
   C. Only the poor
   D. All sections of society

1. D	2. B	3. A	4. C	5. D

8.6 DRUG ABUSE AND TRAFFICKING

1. What is drug abuse?

   A. Legal consumption of substances
   B. Consuming substances without medical approval
   C. Eating healthy food
   D. Regular exercise

2. Which measure is important for dealing with drug abuse?

   A. Ignoring addicts
   B. Legalizing all drugs
   C. Encouraging drug use
   D. Providing proper care and attention

3. Who should play a key role in teaching addicts to avoid drugs?

   A. Politicians
   B. Athletes
   C. Physicians
   D. Celebrities

4. What should parents provide to prevent drug abuse?

   A. Neglect
   B. Strict discipline
   C. Financial support
   D. Care and attention

5. Reading what type of books is helpful for addicts?

   A. Fictional novels
   B. Moral and religious books
   C. Science fiction
   D. Comic books

1. B	2. D	3. C	4. D	5. B

8.7 HIV/AIDS

1. What does HIV stand for?

   A. Human Immuno-deficiency Virus
   B. Human Infectious Virus
   C. Human Immune Virus
   D. Human Immunization Virus

2. How does HIV/AIDS primarily spread?

   A. Through casual contact
   B. Through air
   C. By sharing food
   D. Unprotected sex

3. Which body fluids contain the highest concentration of HIV?

   A. Sweat and saliva
   B. Blood, semen, and vaginal fluids
   C. Tears and urine
   D. None of these

4. What is the term used for the period between the entry of HIV in the body and detection of its antibodies?

   A. Window period
   B. Latent period
   C. Incubation period
   D. Dormant period

5. How can mother-to-child transmission of HIV occur?

   A. During pregnancy
   B. During breastfeeding
   C. During delivery
   D. All of the above

1. A	2. D	3. B	4. A	5. D

8.8 BETI BACHAO BETI PADHAO

1. What is the aim of the Beti Bachao Beti Padhao campaign?

   A. Promote male child education
   B. Generate awareness and improve welfare services for girls

C. Increase female employment
D. Promote technology use in schools

2. Which ministry is NOT involved in the Beti Bachao Beti Padhao campaign?

   A. Ministry of Women and Child Development
   B. Ministry of Health and Family Welfare
   C. Ministry of Human Resource Development
   D. Ministry of Finance

3. When was the trend of declining female population first noticed in India?

   A. 1991 census
   B. 2011 census
   C. 2001 census
   D. 1981 census

4. What is a major cause for the decline in female population?

   A. Poor education
   B. Lack of technology
   C. Dowry system
   D. Government policies

5. The Beti Bachao campaign is supported by which organization?

   A. United Nations
   B. World Bank
   C. World Health Organization
   D. Indian Medical Association

1. B	2. D	3. A	4. C	5. D

8.9 MISSION INDRADHANUSH

1. What is the goal of Mission Indradhanush?

   A. Promote higher education
   B. Achieve full immunization for children by 2020
   C. Increase economic growth
   D. Enhance technological advancements

2. Which disease is NOT targeted by Mission Indradhanush?

   A. Polio
   B. Hepatitis B
   C. Diabetes
   D. Measles

3. Mission Indradhanush was launched in which year?

   A. 2010 B. 2012 C. 2014 D. 2016

4. Who is the primary target group for Mission Indradhanush?

   A. Elderly people
   B. Infants and children under 2 years
   C. Teenagers
   D. Adults over 50 years

5. Which ministry is responsible for implementing Mission Indradhanush?

   A. Ministry of Finance
   B. Ministry of Health and Family Welfare
   C. Ministry of Education
   D. Ministry of Defence

1. B	2. C	3. C	4. B	5. B

8.10 ENVIRONMENTAL ISSUES

1. What is the primary cause of global warming?

   A. Increased use of renewable energy
   B. Deforestation and burning of fossil fuels
   C. Conservation of wildlife
   D. Planting more trees

2. Which gas is most commonly associated with the greenhouse effect?

   A. Oxygen
   B. Hydrogen
   C. Carbon dioxide
   D. Nitrogen

3. Which of the following is a renewable energy source?

   A. Coal
   B. Natural gas
   C. Solar energy
   D. Petroleum

4. What does the term 'biodiversity' refer to?

   A. Variety of living organisms in an area
   B. Various types of weather patterns
   C. Different types of rocks
   D. Different layers of the Earth

5. Which protocol was established to reduce the emission of greenhouse gases?

   A. Kyoto Protocol
   B. Paris Agreement
   C. Geneva Protocol
   D. Montreal Protocol

1. B	2. C	3. C	4. A	5. A

8.11 HUMAN RIGHTS

1. Which document is considered the cornerstone of international human rights law?

   A. Declaration of Independence
   B. Treaty of Versailles
   C. Magna Carta
   D. Universal Declaration of Human Rights

2. Who is responsible for protecting human rights within a country?

   A. International organizations
   B. Neighboring countries
   C. The national government
   D. Corporations

3. What is the right to freedom of speech classified as?

   A. Economic right
   B. Social right
   C. Civil right
   D. Cultural right

4. Which organization is known for advocating for human rights worldwide?

   A. World Bank
   B. United Nations
   C. International Monetary Fund
   D. World Trade Organization

5. What does the right to education ensure?

   A. Free speech
   B. Voting rights
   C. Access to healthcare
   D. Access to free primary education

1. D	2. C	3. C	4. B	5. D

8.12 CHILD LABOUR

1. What is the legal minimum age for employment in most countries?

   A. 12 years B. 14 years C. 16 years D. 18 years

2. Which international organization works to eliminate child labour?

   A. UNESCO B. WHO C. ILO D. IMF

3. What is a major cause of child labour?

   A. High educational standards
   B. Government policies
   C. Economic poverty
   D. High wages

4. Which sector employs the highest number of child labourers?

   A. Technology C. Healthcare
   B. Agriculture D. Education

5. What is an effective measure to combat child labour?

   A. Increasing working hours for children
   B. Improving access to quality education
   C. Encouraging child employment
   D. Reducing adult wages

1. D	2. C	3. C	4. B	5. B

8.13 WOMEN'S RIGHTS

1. What does gender equality ensure?

   A. Equal rights and opportunities for all genders
   B. Higher wages for men
   C. Dominance of one gender over the other
   D. Separate schools for boys and girls

2. Which movement is associated with women's suffrage?

   A. Civil Rights Movement
   B. Feminist Movement
   C. Environmental Movement
   D. Labour Movement

3. What is a common form of violence against women?

   A. Equal pay
   B. Higher education
   C. Domestic violence
   D. Political participation

4. Which international day is dedicated to women's rights?

   A. International Men's Day
   B. International Women's Day

C. Earth Day
D. Human Rights Day

5. What is the goal of Women's Reservation Bill in India?

A. Increase women's participation in the workforce
B. Ensure women's representation in Parliament
C. Promote women in sports
D. Provide financial aid to women

1. A	2. B	3. C	4. B	5. B

8.14 PROTECTION OF CHILDREN AND WOMEN SAFETY

1. What year did the Protection of Children from Sexual Offences (POCSO) Act come into force?

A. 2010 B. 2011 C. 2012 D. 2013

2. According to the POCSO Act, who is defined as a child?

A. Any person below 18 years
B. Any person below 21 years
C. Any person below 16 years
D. Any person below 14 years

3. Which section of the POCSO Act deals with penetrative sexual assault?

A. Section 3
B. Section 5
C. Section 7
D. Section 9

4. Under the POCSO Act, which body is responsible for the periodic monitoring of the provisions of the Act?

    I. National Commission for Women (NCW)
    II. State Commissions for Women (SCW)
    III. National Commission for Protection of Child Rights (NCPCR)
    IV. State Commissions for Protection of Child Rights (SCPCR)

    A. I and II
    B. III and IV
    C. I and III
    D. II and IV

5. What is the minimum punishment for aggravated penetrative sexual assault under the POCSO Act?

    A. Five years imprisonment
    B. Life imprisonment
    C. Seven years imprisonment
    D. Ten years imprisonment

6. What is the age definition of a child under the POCSO Act 2012?

    A. Below 18 years
    B. Below 14 years
    C. Below 16 years
    D. Below 21 years

7. The POCSO Act is __________.

    A. Gender-specific
    B. For boys only
    C. For girls only
    D. Gender-neutral

8. Which section of the POCSO Act deals with Penetrative Sexual Assault?

    A. Section 3
    B. Section 5
    C. Section 7
    D. Section 9

9. What is the minimum punishment for Penetrative Sexual Assault under the POCSO Act?

   A. Three years imprisonment
   B. Seven years imprisonment
   C. Five years imprisonment
   D. Life imprisonment

10. Which section of the POCSO Act addresses the use of a child for pornographic purposes?

   A. Section 3
   B. Section 11
   C. Section 13
   D. Section 15

11. What role does the National Commission for Protection of Child Rights (NCPCR) play under the POCSO Act?

   A. Monitoring the implementation
   B. Conducting trials
   C. Providing legal assistance
   D. All of the above

12. Under the POCSO Act, the medical examination of a child victim must be conducted in the presence of ________.

   A. A police officer
   B. School teachers
   C. Parents or guardians
   D. Social workers

13. Which section of the POCSO Act deals with Sexual Harassment of the Child?

   A. Section 7
   B. Section 9
   C. Section 11
   D. Section 13

14. In which year the POCSO Act came into force?

A. 2010 B. 2011 C. 2012 D. 2013

1. C	2. A	3. A	4. B	5. D	6. A	7. D	8. A	9. B	10. C
11. A	12. C	13. C	14. C						

8.15 CHILD ABUSE

1. What is child abuse defined as?

A. Physical injury to a child
B. Sexual abuse or exploitation of a child
C. Emotional ill-treatment of a child
D. All of the above

2. Which age group of children is most at risk of abuse according to the 2006 national study?

A. 0-4 years C. 13-18 years
B. 5-12 years D. 19-24 years

3. What percentage of children reported facing sexual abuse in the 2006 study?

A. 25% B. 35% C. 53.22% D. 65.40%

4. Child neglect is defined as an act leading to the denial of a child's __________.

A. Education C. Basic needs
B. Entertainment D. Toys

5. In the national study on child abuse in India conducted in 2006, what percentage of children reported facing sexual abuse?

A. 53.22% B. 33.22% C. 43.22% D. 63.22%

6. Which age group is most at risk of abuse and exploitation according to the 2006 national study?

   A. 0-4 years C. 5-12 years
   B. 13-18 years D. 19-24 years

7. Physical abuse involves causing injury by _________.

   A. Ignoring the child
   B. Hitting, shaking, or kicking
   C. Overfeeding
   D. Spoiling

8. Emotional abuse is also known as _________.

   A. Physical abuse C. Sexual abuse
   B. Neglect D. Verbal abuse

9. What is a key sign of emotional abuse?

   A. Mental distress or trauma
   B. Good behaviour
   C. Physical injuries
   D. High academic performance

10. Which form of child abuse involves inappropriate sexual behaviour with a child?

    A. Physical abuse C. Neglect
    B. Emotional abuse D. Sexual abuse

11. Child abuse affects children from which backgrounds?

    A. Only poor families
    B. All religions, castes, and creeds
    C. Only urban areas
    D. Only rural areas

12. Child neglect can lead to the denial of ________.

 A. Basic needs C. Toys
 B. Luxuries D. Pets

13. Which organization conducted the national study on child abuse in India in 2006?

 A. Ministry of Health
 B. Ministry of Child and Women Welfare
 C. Ministry of Education
 D. UNICEF

1. D	2. B	3. C	4. C	5. A	6. C	7. B	8. D	9. A	10. D
11. B	12. A	13. B							

8.16 WOMEN SAFETY

1. Which Act was passed in 1986 to prevent the indecent representation of women?

 A. Dowry Prohibition Act
 B. Indecent Representation of Women (Prevention) Act
 C. Protection of Women from Domestic Violence Act
 D. Sexual Harassment of Women at Workplace Act

2. Which year did the Maternity Benefit Act come into effect?

 A. 1961 B. 1971 C. 1981 D. 1991

3. What is one of the key self-defence techniques recommended for women?

 A. Running away C. Kicks to the groin
 B. Screaming D. Calling the police

4. Which Act provides protection from domestic violence for women?

   A. Child Marriage Restraint Act
   B. Dowry Prohibition Act
   C. Protection of Women from Domestic Violence Act
   D. Equal Remuneration Act

5. In which year was the Equal Remuneration Act enacted?

   A. 1965 B. 1976 C. 1985 D. 1995

6. Which Act prohibits sex selection?

   A. National Commission for Women Act
   B. Prohibition of Sex Selection Act
   C. Maternity Benefit Act
   D. Indecent Representation of Women (Prevention) Act

7. Women generally feel frightened while going alone ________.

   A. To the home
   B. To school
   C. Outside the home
   D. To the office

8. Which of the following is a self-defence technique recommended for women?

   A. Running
   B. Ignoring the attacker
   C. Screaming
   D. Kicks to the groin

9. Women should avoid situations.

   A. Safe B. Pleasant C. Bad D. Boring

10. What should women carry for self-defence?

   A. Pepper spray
   B. A whistle
   C. A flashlight
   D. A book

11. Women should be cautious while _________.

    A. Shopping
    B. Reading
    C. Eating
    D. Communicating on the internet

12. Emergency numbers are important for women to _________.

    A. Memorize
    B. Carry with them
    C. Ignore
    D. Share on social media

13. Women should be careful while _________ a car.

    A. Washing
    B. Painting
    C. Driving
    D. Cleaning

14. Which act is aimed at preventing domestic violence against women?

    A. Protection of Women from Domestic Violence Act
    B. Dowry Prohibition Act
    C. Hindu Marriage Act
    D. Child Marriage Restraint Act

15. The Indecent Representation of Women (Prevention) Act was enacted in _________.

    A. 1986 B. 1990 C. 1994 D. 2005

16. The Sexual Harassment of Women at Workplace Act was enacted in _________.

    A. 2005 B. 2010 C. 2013 D. 2015

1. B	2. A	3. C	4. C	5. B	6. B	7. C	8. D	9. C	10. A
11. D	12. B	13. C	14. A	15. A	16. C				

8.17 ROAD/RAIL TRAVEL SAFETY

1. What should you always carry while traveling by rail?

   A. A map
   B. Identification card
   C. Snacks
   D. Extra money

2. Which one is a 'Don't' for road safety?

   A. Obey traffic rules
   B. Wear helmet and seat belts
   C. Use mobile phones while driving
   D. Educate general public on traffic rules

3. What is the recommended action if you notice unidentified objects or suspected persons in the train?

   A. Ignore it
   B. Report to the railway police
   C. Leave the train immediately
   D. Confront the person

4. Which Act is a significant step in traffic control and anti-drunken driving measures?

   A. The Motor Vehicle Act
   B. The Public Safety Act
   C. The Railways Act
   D. The Traffic Regulation Act

5. What should be the first item to pack for a journey?

   A. Money
   B. Clothes
   C. Common sense
   D. Food

6. What should you do before traveling if you recently had major health problems?

   A. Pack extra medications
   B. Update your immunizations
   C. Get a physical exam
   D. All of the above

7. Which item is essential to carry for safety during travel?

   A. Extra clothes
   B. Travel guide
   C. Identity card
   D. Books

8. Which food-related advice is given for travellers?

   A. Carry lots of snacks
   B. Choose the right food due to limited space
   C. Eat only at restaurants
   D. Avoid carrying food

9. A road accident is also known as a __________ .

   A. Vehicle mishap
   B. Traffic jam
   C. Motor vehicle collision (MVC)
   D. Parking issue

10. A rail accident involving one or more trains is often due to __________.

    A. Miscommunication
    B. Overcrowding
    C. Weather conditions
    D. Long travel distances

11. What is a key measure to prevent road accidents?

    A. Over speeding
    B. Obeying traffic rules
    C. Drinking and driving
    D. Ignoring pedestrians

12. Which of the following is a don't for rail safety?

    A. Using over bridges to cross tracks
    B. Carrying an identification card
    C. Sitting on the footsteps/footboard while traveling
    D. Reporting unidentified objects to railway police

13. What should be avoided while driving to ensure safety?

    A. Wearing seat belts
    B. Using mobile phones
    C. Following traffic signals
    D. Attending road safety seminars

14. In case of an emergency on a train, one should __________.

    A. Panic
    B. Jump off the train
    C. Ignore it
    D. Pull the chain

15. Which organization plays a key role in rail safety in India?

    A. Indian Railways
    B. Ministry of Education
    C. Indian Army
    D. Ministry of Environment

16. Using seat belts while driving helps to __________.

    A. Increase speed
    B. Save fuel
    C. Improve visibility
    D. Reduce the risk of injury

17. What is the purpose of pedestrian crossings?

A. Parking vehicles
B. Road construction
C. Pedestrian safety
D. Traffic management

18. Which of the following is important for vehicle maintenance?

A. Ignoring small repairs
B. Overloading the vehicle
C. Regular servicing
D. Avoiding tire checks

1. B	2. C	3. B	4. A	5. C	6. D	7. C	8. B	9. C	10. A
11. B	12. C	13. B	14. D	15. A	16. D	17. C	18. C		

8.18 NEW INITIATIVES

1. Which app is used for fast, safe, and trustworthy payments in India?

A. Google Pay
B. Paytm
C. BHIM App
D. PhonePe

2. Which initiative encourages manufacturing in India?

A. Make in India
B. Skill India
C. Start-up India
D. Digital India

3. What is the purpose of the Mudra Bank?

A. Provide education loans
B. Provide agricultural loans
C. Provide loans for housing
D. Provide loans for entrepreneurs

4. Which initiative is aimed at providing skill training schemes?

   A. Digital India
   B. Skill India
   C. Make in India
   D. Star-tup India

5. What is the main goal of the Aadhar initiative?

   A. Provide financial assistance
   B. Promote education
   C. Unique identity for citizens
   D. Encourage entrepreneurship

6. Which initiative encourages new businessmen?

   A. Make in India
   B. Start-up India
   C. Skill India
   D. Digital India

7. Which act was passed to lower the juvenile age from 18 to 16 years in cases of heinous offenses?

   A. Indian Penal Code
   B. Juvenile Justice (Care and Protection of Children) Act 2000
   C. Juvenile Justice (Care and Protection of Children) Bill 2015
   D. National Commission for Women Act

1. C	2. A	3. D	4. B	5. C	6. B	7. C

8.19 DISASTER MANAGEMENT

1. Disaster management involves __________.

   A. Planning and response
   B. Creating disasters
   C. Ignoring disasters
   D. Preventing accidents

2. Which of the following is NOT a type of natural disaster?

   A. Earthquake
   B. Flood
   C. Fire
   D. Tsunami

3. The National Disaster Management Authority (NDMA) is headed by __________.

   A. The President of India
   B. The Prime Minister of India
   C. The Home Minister
   D. The defense minister

4. Which phase in disaster management focuses on long-term measures to reduce or eliminate risk?

   A. Preparedness
   B. Mitigation
   C. Response
   D. Recovery

5. The key objective of disaster preparedness is to __________.

   A. Minimize the impact
   B. Enhance recovery efforts
   C. Create awareness
   D. Conduct mock drills

6. Which of the following is a man-made disaster?

   A. Tornado
   B. Cyclone
   C. Chemical spill
   D. Landslide

7. Evacuation plans are part of _________ in disaster management.

   A. Mitigation
   B. Response
   C. Recovery
   D. Preparedness

8. The term 'hazard' refers to _________.

   A. Safe zones
   B. Emergency responders
   C. Potential sources of harm
   D. Relief measures

9. Which agency is responsible for disaster management at the state level in India?

   A. NDMA
   B. SDRF
   C. NDRF
   D. Police Department

10. An example of a structural measure for disaster mitigation is _________.

    A. Building earthquake-resistant structures
    B. Public awareness campaigns
    C. Early warning systems
    D. Conducting training programs

1. A	2. C	3. B	4. B	5. A	6. C	7. D	8. C	9. B	10. A

8.20 ELECTRICAL SAFETY

1. Electrical hazards can cause _________.

   A. Injuries
   B. Fires
   C. Fatalities
   D. All of the above

2. Which of the following is a common cause of electrical accidents?

   A. Proper insulation
   B. Overloading circuits
   C. Grounded equipment
   D. Regular maintenance

3. Grounding is important because it _________.

   A. Increases voltage
   B. Prevents current flow
   C. Causes short circuits
   D. Provides a path for electric current

4. Which safety device cuts off the power supply in case of a fault?

   A. Light switch
   B. Circuit breaker
   C. Bulb
   D. Battery

5. One should never handle electrical equipment with_________.

   A. Wet hands
   B. Clean hands
   C. Dry hands
   D. Gloves

6. The color code for a live wire in electrical wiring is _________.

   A. Green
   B. Blue
   C. Brown or Red
   D. Black

7. Which material is a good insulator?

   A. Copper
   B. Aluminum
   C. Plastic
   D. Steel

8. Electrical appliances should be ________ when not in use.

   A. Turned off
   B. Left on
   C. Ignored
   D. Covered with cloth

9. The purpose of a fuse in an electrical circuit is to ________.

   A. Increase current flow
   B. Break the circuit in case of overload
   C. Supply additional power
   D. Store electricity

10. Which of the following should NOT be done during an electrical fire?

    A. Use water to extinguish
    B. Turn off the power source
    C. Use a fire extinguisher
    D. Evacuate the area

1. D	2. B	3. D	4. B	5. A	6. C	7. C	8. A	9. B	10. A

8.21 CYBER SAFETY

1. Cyber safety involves protecting against ________.

   A. Online threats
   B. Natural disasters
   C. Physical theft
   D. Traffic accidents

2. Phishing is a type of cyber-attack that involves __________.

   A. Sending unsolicited emails
   B. Stealing personal information
   C. Creating fake websites
   D. All of the above

3. Which of the following is a strong password example?

   A. 12345
   B. Password
   C. MySecure@1234
   D. ABCD

4. Two-factor authentication adds __________ to the security process.

   A. Another layer of protection
   B. Convenience
   C. Complexity
   D. More users

5. The term 'malware' refers to __________.

   A. Legitimate software
   B. Malicious software
   C. Hardware devices
   D. Data encryption

6. Which of the following is NOT a common type of malware?

   A. Virus
   B. Trojan
   C. Firewall
   D. Ransomware

7. A firewall helps to __________.

   A. Protect a network from unauthorized access
   B. Increase internet speed
   C. Create websites
   D. Store data securely

8. Which of the following is an example of identity theft?

   A. Using someone else's credit card information
   B. Sending spam emails
   C. Encrypting data
   D. Installing software updates

9. Which of the following is a safe online behaviour?

   A. Sharing personal information publicly
   B. Using the same password for multiple accounts
   C. Regularly updating passwords
   D. Clicking on unknown links

10. Which organization is responsible for cyber security in India?

    A. CERT-In B. RBI C. NDMA D. SEBI

1. A	2. D	3. C	4. A	5. B	6. C	7. A	8. A	9. C	10. A

8.22 EMERGENCY RESPONSE

1. The first step in emergency response is to __________.

   A. Panic
   B. Assess the situation
   C. Run away
   D. Ignore the emergency

2. CPR stands for _________.

   A. Critical Patient Rescue
   B. Cardiac Pulmonary Recovery
   C. Cardiopulmonary Resuscitation
   D. Continuous Patient Relief

3. Which of the following is NOT a part of the emergency response plan?

   A. Preparedness
   B. Training
   C. Ignorance
   D. Communication

4. In an emergency, the most important thing is to _________.

   A. Stay calm
   B. Shout loudly
   C. Run fast
   D. Hide away

5. Emergency contact numbers should be _________.

   A. Forgotten
   B. Ignored
   C. Stored and accessible
   D. Shared on social media

6. What is the purpose of an emergency drill?

   A. To create panic
   B. To increase fear
   C. To waste time
   D. To test and improve response

7. Which emergency service is called for medical emergencies?

   A. Fire service
   B. Police
   C. Ambulance
   D. National Guard

8. The universal emergency number in many countries is __________.

   A. 911 B. 123 C. 789 D. 555

9. In case of a fire emergency, one should __________.

   A. Use elevators
   B. Use stairs
   C. Hide under a table
   D. Open all windows

10. An emergency response team (ERT) is __________.

    A. A group of volunteers
    B. Only for large organizations
    C. Formed for fun activities
    D. Trained to respond to emergencies

1. B	2. C	3. C	4. A	5. C	6. D	7. C	8. A	9. B	10. D

8.23 GENERAL SAFETY

1. Safety is defined as __________.

   A. The absence of risk
   B. A feeling of fear
   C. Ignorance of danger
   D. Freedom from injury or harm

2. What should be the first step in risk assessment?

   A. Identify hazards
   B. Implement solutions
   C. Ignore risks
   D. Monitor the environment

3. Which of the following is NOT a personal protective equipment (PPE)?

   A. Gloves
   B. Helmets
   C. Sunglasses
   D. Safety boots

4. Which of the following is a proactive safety measure?

   A. Waiting for an accident to happen
   B. Regular safety training
   C. Ignoring safety protocols
   D. Not using PPE

5. Safety signs are used to ________ .

   A. Confuse people
   B. Decorate the workplace
   C. Provide information and warnings
   D. Waste resources

6. A near miss is an event ________ .

   A. That results in injury
   B. That could have caused injury or damage but did not
   C. That causes a fatality
   D. That has no impact at all

7. Which of the following is an example of an ergonomic hazard?

   A. Repetitive movements
   B. Chemical spills
   C. Noise exposure
   D. Fire

8. Which act governs occupational health and safety in India?

   A. The Factories Act, 1948
   B. The Income Tax Act, 1961
   C. The Companies Act, 2013
   D. The Environmental Protection Act, 1986

9. Slips, trips, and falls are examples of ________ hazards.

   A. Chemical
   B. Physical
   C. Biological
   D. Psychological

10. What is the main goal of workplace safety programs?

    A. To increase production
    B. To ensure the health and safety of employees
    C. To improve marketing
    D. To reduce salaries

1. D	2. A	3. C	4. B	5. C	6. B	7. A	8. A	9. B	10. B

8.24 FIRE SAFETY

1. The fire triangle consists of ________.

   A. Water, air, and fuel
   B. Earth, wind, and fire
   C. Heat, fuel, and oxygen
   D. Heat, light, and sound

2. Which of the following is a Class A fire?

   A. Electrical fires
   B. Fires involving flammable liquids
   C. Fires involving ordinary combustibles like wood and paper
   D. Fires involving metals

3. A fire extinguisher suitable for electrical fires is __________.

   A. Water-based
   B. CO2-based
   C. Foam-based
   D. Metal-based

4. The PASS technique in using a fire extinguisher stands for __________.

   A. Pull, Aim, Squeeze, Sweep
   B. Pull, Alert, Sweep, Squeeze
   C. Push, Alert, Squeeze, Sweep
   D. Push, Aim, Sweep, Squeeze

5. Which of the following should NOT be used on a grease fire?

   A. Water
   B. Fire extinguisher
   C. Baking soda
   D. Lid to cover the fire

6. Which type of smoke detector uses a small amount of radioactive material?

   A. Photoelectric smoke detector
   B. Carbon monoxide detector

C. Heat detector
D. Ionization smoke detector

7. What is the first thing you should do if you discover a fire?

A. Try to put it out
B. Raise the alarm
C. Run away
D. Hide

8. In case of a fire, you should _________.

A. Use the elevator
B. Open all windows
C. Stay low to avoid smoke
D. Gather belongings

9. Which organization sets fire safety standards in India?

A. BIS
B. RBI
C. NDMA
D. SEBI

10. An assembly point is _________ .

A. A place where people gather during a fire emergency
B. The location of the fire
C. The fire extinguisher storage area
D. The area where fire trucks are parked

1. C	2. C	3. B	4. A	5. A	6. D	7. B	8. C	9. A	10. A

09

Health and Hygiene

9.1 HYGIENE AND SANITATION (PERSONAL AND CAMP)

1. What is the objective of maintaining hygiene?

   A. Preventing the development and spread of infections
   B. Making cadets aware of preventable health hazards
   C. To developing concepts of healthy living
   D. All of the above

2. Who is responsible for maintaining personal health?

   A. Yoga trainer
   B. Doctors
   C. The individual
   D. Army training

3. How many hours of sleep recommend for an average individual?

   A. 5 to 6 hours
   B. 7 to 8 hours
   C. 9 to 10 hours
   D. 10 to 12 hours

4. Which of the following is NOT a component of personal hygiene?

   A. Handwashing
   B. Hair care
   C. Nail painting
   D. Oral hygiene

5. What is the purpose of brushing teeth?

   A. To prevent bad breath
   B. To prevent tooth decay

C. To prevent gum diseases
D. All of the above

6. __________ is important for preventing Athlete's foot?

A. Bathing regularly
B. Keeping finger and toe nails trimmed and dry
C. Washing hands frequently
D. Maintaining proper sleep patterns

7. Food hygiene is concerned with __________?

A. Safety of food from production to consumption
B. Safety of food from storage to preparation
C. Safety of food from processing to distribution
D. Safety of food from harvesting to transportation

8. Lack of adequate food hygiene lead to_________.

A. Food shortages and starvation
B. Higher food prices
C. Food poisoning and death
D. Rice in food production costs

9. What is the primary goal of personal hygiene practices?

A. Promoting social interactions
B. Preventing the spread of disease
C. Enhancing physical strength
D. Increasing mental alertness

10. Which of the following is NOT a key to safer food?

A. Keep clean
B. Use safe and clean water and raw materials
C. Cook thoroughly
D. Consume food within 24 hours

11. The important components of food hygiene are _________.

    A. Cooking and serving
    B. Production to handling and distribution and serving
    C. Storage and distribution
    D. Cleaning and sanitizing

12. Which of the following is NOT a method to ensure food hygiene during preparation?

    A. Using separate cutting boards
    B. Washing raw ingredients thoroughly
    C. Cooking food with dirty utensils
    D. Storing food at appropriate temperatures

13. How should milk vessels be treated to prevent contamination?

    A. Left uncovered
    B. Cleaned and sanitized
    C. Regularly replaced
    D. Exposed to sunlight

14. What should milk handlers ensure before the milking process?

    A. Animal vaccination
    B. Personal protective gear
    C. Clean surroundings
    D. Proper ventilation

15. Who should handle milk?

    A. Any individual trained in milking technique
    B. Anyone willing to do
    C. Those who are free from any communicable disease
    D. Those with proper authorization

16. Where can food become contaminated?

    A. Only during harvesting
    B. At any point from production to consumption
    C. Only during transportation
    D. Only during preparation

17. What is the primary purpose of maintaining food hygiene?

    A. To increase food production
    B. To ensure food tastes good
    C. To prevent foodborne illnesses
    D. To reduce food wastage

18. What is the main reason for ensuring a safe water supply in food hygiene?

    A. To enhance the taste of food
    B. To prevent contamination during cooking
    C. To minimize the risk of foodborne diseases
    D. To reduce food production costs

19. What does food hygiene primarily focus on?

    A. Taste enhancement
    B. Safety from contamination
    C. Aesthetic presentation
    D. Nutritional value

20. What is emphasized as important during the handling of food to prevent contamination?

    A. Frequent tasting
    B. Using bare hands
    C. Wearing gloves
    D. Avoiding handwashing

21. What is pasteurization?

    A. Altering the taste of milk
    B. Increasing the nutritive value of milk
    C. Enhancing the color of milk
    D. Sterilization of milk

22. Which of the following is recommended as essential for fish intended for human consumption?

    I. Brightly colored scales
    II. Clear and prominent eyes
    III. Sharp teeth
    IV. Slimy texture

    A. I and II
    B. III and IV
    C. II and III
    D. I and IV

23. How does eggs are contaminated?

    A. Through airborne pathogens
    B. By exposure to sunlight
    C. Through contact with faecal matter
    D. By food given to the hen

24. What is the recommended practice before cooking eggs?

    A. Heating the eggs to high temperatures
    B. Applying a chemical disinfectant
    C. Properly washing the eggs
    D. Using only organic eggs

25. Why it is important to wash fruits and vegetables before consumption?

    A. To remove potential pathogens
    B. To increase their shelf-life

C. To enhance their flavor
D. To preserve their natural color

26. Which of the following is NOT considered for maintaining hygiene in eating places?

    A. Proximity to open drains
    B. Availability of Wi-Fi
    C. Proper lighting and ventilation
    D. Separation of perishable and non-perishable items

27. Sanitation primarily involves________.

    A. Cooking techniques
    B. Water purification methods
    C. Food storage practices
    D. Waste removal and cleanliness

28. What is the main concern regarding food quality in camps?

    A. Availability of exotic dishes
    B. Decorative presentation of meal
    C. Prevention of food poisoning
    D. Usage of organic ingredients

29. How long should a sample of food provided to cadets be preserved after serving?

    A. 12 hours
    B. 24 hours
    C. 36 hours
    D. 48 hours

30. Ideal reason for all food preparation preliminaries made in a separate room?

    A. To save time
    B. To prevent cross-contamination
    C. To minimize food waste
    D. To maintain proper ventilation

31. The recommended condition for serving cooked food is_________.

    A. Cold
    B. Lukewarm
    C. Hot
    D. Room temperature

32. What should be regularly inspected in the cook house?

    A. Cadets' attire
    B. Hygiene, sanitation, and cleanliness
    C. Cooks' footwear
    D. Kitchen decorations

33. What is the purpose of maintaining hygiene and sanitation in cookhouses?

    A. To impress visitors
    B. To prevent foodborne illnesses
    C. To comply with regulations
    D. To reduce cooking time

34. What is the purpose of soakage pits in a camp?

    A. To store water for drinking purposes
    B. To dispose of waste food
    C. To provide drainage for rainwater
    D. To bury waste material and prevent breeding of flies

35. Water used in the camp should be________.

    A. It should be sourced from natural springs only with algae
    B. It must be from authorized source and certified as potable by local medical authorities
    C. It should be treated with chemicals before use
    D. It should be stored in uncovered containers for easy access

36. What type of latrine is suitable for camps of less than a week's duration?

    A. Deep Trench Latrines (DTLs)
    B. Shallow Trench Latrines
    C. Urinals
    D. RO plant latrines

37. What is the recommended practice for the disposal of excreta in shallow trench latrines?

    A. Filling up the trenches with soil after 24 hours
    B. Leaving the excreta exposed to air for natural decomposition
    C. Covering the excreta with plastic sheets
    D. Dumping the excreta in nearby water bodies

38. How should latrines be maintained in the camp?

    A. By leaving them uncleaned to encourage natural decomposition
    B. By washing wooden frames twice, a day and treating them with lime
    C. By removing partition screens for easier access
    D. By minimizing the number of urinals to reduce maintenance efforts

9.2 FIRST AID IN COMMON MEDICAL EMERGENCIES AND TREATMENT OF WOUNDS

1. What is the aim/objective of first aid?

   A. To provide definitive medical treatment
   B. To prevent injury or illness
   C. To save life and prevent the condition from worsening
   D. To administer medication

2. Which of the following animal bite causes Rabies?

   A. Cat B. Rat C. Dog D. Bat

3. DTL stand for __________

   A. Dangerous Target Location
   B. Drainage To locate
   C. Deep Trench Location
   D. Deep Trench Latrine

4. RMO stands for__________

   A. Regional Medical Officer
   B. Regional Manager Office
   C. Regional Medical Outlet
   D. Regional Media Official

5. Which test is done for detection of AIDS?

   A. HMV C. H1N1
   B. HPV D. HIV

6. Full form of AIDS is _________.

   A. Acquired Immune Deficiency Syndrome
   B. Autoimmune Immunodeficiency Syndrome

C. Acquired Immune Detection System
D. Anti-Immune Deficiency Syndrome

7. Which virus is responsible for causing AIDS?

A. Influenza virus
B. Herpes virus
C. Hepatitis virus
D. Human Immunodeficiency Virus (HIV)

8. How is HIV primarily transmitted?

A. Airborne droplets
B. Sexual contact
C. Mosquito bites
D. Casual contact like shaking hands

9. Which of the following bodily fluids is NOT considered a common mode of HIV transmission?

A. Blood
B. Semen
C. Saliva
D. Vaginal fluids

10. What is the most common method for preventing the spread of HIV?

A. Using condoms during sexual activity
B. Eating a healthy diet
C. Avoiding vaccinations
D. Taking daily vitamins

11. Which of the following statements about HIV/AIDS is TRUE?

    A. There is currently a vaccine available for HIV.
    B. HIV can be completely cured with antibiotics.
    C. HIV/AIDS primarily affects older adults.
    D. HIV weakens the immune system, making it difficult for the body to fight off infections.

12. Which population group is most affected by HIV/AIDS globally?

    A. Children under 5 years old
    B. Adolescents and young adults
    C. Middle-aged adults
    D. Elderly people

13. Which of the following is the correct description of a heartbeat?

    A. The contraction of the heart muscle
    B. The expansion of the lungs
    C. The relaxation of the heart muscle
    D. The flow of blood through the veins

14. What is the average resting heart rate for adults?

    A. 60-80 beats per minute
    B. 40-50 beats per minute
    C. 100-120 beats per minute
    D. 20-30 beats per minute

15. What is the name of the electrical signal that initiates a heartbeat?

    A. Synapse
    B. Action potential
    C. Pulse
    D. Pacemaker

16. Which chamber of the heart pumps oxygen-rich blood to the rest of the body?

A. Left atrium
B. Right atrium
C. Left ventricle
D. Right ventricle

17. What term is used to describe an irregular heartbeat?

A. Tachycardia
B. Bradycardia
C. Arrhythmia
D. Murmur

18. Which of the following factors can influence heart rate?

A. Altitude
B. Blood type
C. Hair color
D. Shoe size

19. What is the maximum number of times the heart can beat in one minute?

A. 70beats/min
B. 72beats/min
C. 90beats/min
D. 102beats/min

20. What is the primary function of the heart's valves?

A. To regulate blood pressure
B. To produce red blood cells
C. To prevent the backflow of blood
D. To regulate body temperature

21. How many bones are there in human body?

A. 200 B. 204 C. 206 D. 210

22. __________ are the blood vessels which carry pure blood from heart

A. Capillaries B. Veins C. Nerves D. Arteries

23. Which human organ removes/filters waste material in the form of urine?

A. Kidney
B. Liver
C. Lungs
D. Pancreas

24. Other than kidney which human organ removes/filters waste material from body

A. Stomach
B. Ear
C. Skin
D. Eyes

25. Which of the following is a water borne disease?

A. TB
B. AIDS
C. Cancer
D. Dysentery

26. Displacement of one or more bone at joint is called

A. Fracture
B. Sprain
C. Dislocation
D. Strain

27. Purification of water by chlorine gas or bleaching powder is called ________.

A. Chlorination
B. Sedimentation
C. Coagulation
D. Precipitation

28. Alum is used in ________

A. Sterilization
B. Pinking
C. Precipitation
D. Clarification

29. ________ spreads plague

A. Lice
B. Mosquitos
C. Fleas
D. Rat

30. Which of the following is a vector of spreading plague?

A. Lice
B. Mosquitos
C. Fleas
D. Rat

31. Bones confined to upper and lower limbs are

A. Short bones
B. Long bones
C. Flat bone
D. Wrinkled bones

32. TAB stands for or TAB vaccine protect against ________.

A. Tuberculosis, Anthrax, and Botulism
B. Typhoid, Anthrax, and BCG
C. Tetanus, Anthrax, and Botulism
D. Tetanus, Anthrax, and BCG

33. ________ is caused by damage to a blood vessel that in turn causes blood to collect under the skin.

A. Hematomas
B. Keratomas
C. Hepatomas
D. Nematoma

34. Petechiae, purpura, and ecchymosis are types of ________

A. Hematomas
B. Keratomas
C. Hepatomas
D. Nematoma

35. Anything which interferes with respiration producing irregularities in breathing, produces a condition known as ________

A. Aphasia
B. Asphyxia
C. Dysphasia
D. Dyslexia

36. Drowning, Hanging/Strangulation and Suffocation results in ________

A. Aphasia
B. Asphyxia
C. Dysphasia
D. Dyslexia

37. In rabies, dog and the patient should be kept under observation for at least _________ days.

A. 10 B. 15 C. 7 D. 12

38. The Mission Indradhanush is _________

A. Army operations at Ladakh
B. Eradicate illiteracy
C. Immunization/Vaccination to children
D. Empowering youth

39. Lemon is a rich source of _________ vitamin.

A. A B. B C. C D. D

40. Malaria, Chicken gunia are spread by_________

A. Mosquitoes
B. Housefly
C. Water
D. Worms

41. The color of blood is red due to _________pigment

A. Leg hemoglobin
B. Red blood cells
C. Anthocyanin
D. Hemoglobin

42. _________ affects lungs of human body.

A. Diabetes
B. Malaria
C. Pneumonia
D. Arthritis

43. Conjunctivitis is a disease of _________

A. Stomach B. Eyes C. Ears D. Brain

44. Saliva helps in _________

A. Digestion
B. Vision
C. Respiration
D. Hearing

45. Any healthy person between age of _________ can donate blood.

A. 16-45 years
B. 18-60 years
C. 21-50 years
D. 25-55 years

46. _________ is the longest bone in human body.

A. Femur
B. Tibia
C. Fibula
D. Humerus

47. Which of the following is the smallest bone in the human body?

A. Femur
B. Tibia
C. Stapes
D. Radius

48. _________ is the largest organ in the human body.

A. Liver
B. Skin
C. Brain
D. Lungs

49. _________ is the weight of human brain.

A. 1.3 to 1.4Kg
B. 2Kg
C. 1.1 to 1.2Kg
D. 1.6Kg

50. What is the source of Vitamin D?

A. Citrus fruits
B. Dairy products
C. Sunlight
D. Leafy green vegetables

51. HIV affects _________ system of human body.

A. Immune
B. Nervous
C. Muscular
D. Skeletal

52. True universal donor blood group is ________.

A. AB^{-ve} B. O^{+ve} C. O^{-ve} D. AB^{+ve}

53. True universal acceptor blood group is ________.

A. AB^{-ve} B. O^{+ve} C. O^{-ve} D. AB^{+ve}

54. _________ is a water borne disease.

A. Jaundice
B. Cholera
C. Giardia
D. All of these

55. Holger-Nielson method is a type of _________

A. Shock treatment
B. Artificial respiration
C. Wound bandaging
D. Backache relief

56. Oxygenated blood is carried by _________ and deoxygenated blood by_________

A. Arteries and Veins
B. Veins and Arteries
C. Both by Arteries
D. Both by Veins

57. In which country the concepts and practices of Yoga is originated?

A. Japan B. China C. Srilanka D. India

58. What is first Aid?

A. The assistance given to any person suffering a sudden illness or injury
B. The assistance given to any person going to attend interview
C. The assistance given to any person suffering from psychological problems
D. The assistance given to any person suffering from genetic disorders

59. Which articles are required for dressing wounds?

A. Anti-septic lotion.
B. Cotton gauze
C. Scissors
D. All of these

60. Boiling, filtration, sedimentation, chlorination and distillation are of _________ purification techniques.

A. Blood
B. Water
C. Air
D. Soil

61. Malaria, Dengue, Chickengunya and zika virus are transmitted by _________

A. House fly
B. Aerosols
C. Contaminated water
D. Mosquitos

62. Match the following for type of wound and causing object

Type of wound	Causing object
1. Incisions.	A. Clean, sharp-edged object
2. Lacerations.	B. Blunt instrument
3. Abrasions (Grazes).	C. Sliding fall onto a rough surface
4. Avulsions	D. A body structure is forcibly detached from its normal point of insertion.
5. Puncture Wounds	E. A splinter, nail or needle.
6. Penetration Wounds	F. Knife

A. 1A, 2B, 3D, 4C, 5F, 6E
B. 1G, 2F, 3E, 4D, 5C, 6B
C. 1B, 2C, 3A, 4D, 5F, 6E
D. 1A, 2B, 3C, 4D, 5E, 6F

63. Which of the following best describes the pulmonary vein?

    A. Carries deoxygenated blood to the lungs
    B. Carries oxygenated blood from the heart to the body
    C. Carries oxygenated blood from the lungs to the heart
    D. Carries deoxygenated blood from the body to the heart

64. Which of the following best describes the pulmonary artery?

    A. Carries deoxygenated blood to the lungs
    B. Carries oxygenated blood from the heart to the body
    C. Carries oxygenated blood from the lungs to the heart
    D. Carries deoxygenated blood from the body to the heart

65. Match the following for vitamins and their function

Vitamin	Function
1. Vitamin A	A. Blood clotting
2. Vitamin K	B. Vision
3. Vitamin D	C. Antioxidant and antisterility
4. Vitamin E	D. Bone health and calcium absorption

A. 1C, 2A, 3D, 4B
B. 1B, 2A, 3D, 4C
C. 1 D, 2C, 3B, 4A
D. 1B, 2C, 3D, 4A

9.3 INTRODUCTION TO YOGA

1. Match the following Yoga asanas and benefits or uses

Yoga Asanas	Benefits or uses
1. Sarvangasana.	A. Circulatory, respiratory and alimentary systems of the body.
2. Halasana	B. Stimulates blood circulation and makes the spine flexible and elastic.
3. Dhanurasana.	C. Good exercise to the abdominal muscles, lower back and thighs,
4. Vajrasana	D. Helps digestion and eliminates gas troubles
5. Shavasana.	E. Releasing the mind from the body
6. Siddhasana.	F. Awaken the power of Kundalini.
7. Padmasana.	G. This asana is useful for Jaap, Dhyana and Samadhi. This asana also helps in curing diseases like asthama, hysteria and insomnia.

A. 1A, 2B, 3C, 4D, 5E, 6F, 7G
B. C. 1B, 2C, 3A, 4D, 5F, 6E, 7G
C. 1G, 2F, 3E, 4D, 5C, 6B, 7A
D. D. 1A, 2B, 3D, 4C, 5F, 6E, 7G

1. D	2. C	3. B	4. C	5. D	6. B	7. A	8. C	9. B	10. D
11. B	12. C	13. B	14. C	15. C	16. B	17. C	18. C	19. B	20. C

21. D	22. A	23. C	24. C	25. A	26. B	27. D	28. C	29. C	30. B
31. C	32. B	33. B	34. D	35. B	36. A	37. A	38. B	39. C	40. C
41. D	42. A	43. D	44. A	45. D	46. B	47. C	48. A	49. D	50. B
51. A	52. A	53. D	54. C	55. C	56. A	57. B	58. C	59. C	60. D
61. A	62. C	63. D	64. C	65. A	66.	67. C	68. D	69.B	70. D
71. A	72. A	73. B	74. B	75. A	76. C	77. C	78. A	79. D	80. C
81. B	82. A	83. B	84. A	85. C	86. B	87. A	88. C	89. A	90. C
91. A	92. D	93. B	94. A	95. D	96. A	97. D	98. B	99. D	100. D
101. C	102. A	103. B	104. A						

10

Adventure

1. Which activity involves climbing steep, rocky terrain?

   A. Hiking
   B. Mountaineering
   C. Bird watching
   D. Fishing

2. What is the aim/focus of adventure tourism?

   A. Relaxation
   B. Education
   C. Excitement and risk
   D. Shopping

3. Which of the following is an example of a water-based adventure activity?

   A. Rock climbing
   B. Paragliding
   C. Mountain biking
   D. Scuba diving

4. What equipment is essential for rock climbing?

   A. Helmet, harness, and ropes
   B. Skis and poles
   C. Fishing rod and bait
   D. Surfboard and wetsuit

5. Which activity requires a parachute?

   A. Surfing
   B. Skydiving
   C. Kayaking
   D. Mountain biking

6. Which of the following is a winter adventure sport?

   A. Sailing
   B. Hiking
   C. Snow surfing
   D. Skiing

7. What is the main appeal of adventure sports?

   A. Low-cost
   B. High safety
   C. Thrill and excitement
   D. Comfort

8. Which activity typically takes place in a desert environment?

   A. Snowboarding
   B. Sandboarding
   C. White-water rafting
   D. Cave diving

9. Which adventure activity involves navigating a river with rapids?

   A. Kayaking
   B. Sailing
   C. Skydiving
   D. Caving

10. What is the risk in adventure sports?

    A. Predictable conditions
    B. Lack of excitement
    C. Controlled environments
    D. Unpredictable elements

11. __________ activity involves riding large ocean waves?

    A. Surfing
    B. Skiing
    C. Hiking
    D. Rock climbing

12. __________ equipment is crucial for scuba diving?

    A. Helmet
    B. Oxygen tank
    C. Harness
    D. Parachute

13. An important safety measure in mountaineering activity is_________.

    A. Lightweight clothing
    B. Ropes and carabiners
    C. Proper hydration
    D. Sandals

14. Which adventure sport is performed on snow-covered slopes?

    A. Surfing B. Kayaking C. Caving D. Skiing

15. What is the main challenge in caving (spelunking)?

    A. Large open spaces
    B. Calm environments
    C. Navigating narrow passages
    D. Warm temperatures

16. Which activity is best suited for exploring underwater ecosystems?

    A. Mountaineering
    B. Scuba diving
    C. Paragliding
    D. Mountain biking

17. What does paragliding involve?

    A. Sailing in the ocean
    B. Exploring caves
    C. Flying using a lightweight glider
    D. Climbing mountains

18. Which activity is commonly done in forested areas?

    A. Surfing
    B. Skydiving
    C. Hiking
    D. Kayaking

19. What is a common feature of adventure sports?

    A. High level of comfort
    B. Adrenaline rush
    C. Predictable outcomes
    D. Low physical activity

20. Which sport involves descending a steep slope on a board?

    A. Rock climbing
    B. Skiing
    C. Caving
    D. Sandboarding

21. Which activity is associated with high altitudes?

    A. Surfing
    B. Mountain biking
    C. Mountaineering
    D. Kayaking

22. Which equipment is essential for safe kayaking?

    A. Helmet and life jacket
    B. Ski poles
    C. Parachute
    D. Climbing harness

23. Which adventure sport involves free-falling from an aircraft?

    A. Rock climbing
    B. Skydiving
    C. Scuba diving
    D. Caving

24. What type of adventure activity is rock climbing?

    A. Water-based
    B. Aerial
    C. Land-based
    D. Snow-based

25. Which adventure sport requires a snow-covered terrain?

    A. Sandboarding
    B. Hiking
    C. Scuba diving
    D. Skiing

1. B	2. C	3. D	4. A	5. B	6. D	7. C	8. A	9. A	10. D
11. A	12. B	13. B	14. D	15. C	16. B	17. C	18. C	19. B	20. D
21. C	22. A	23. B	24. C	25. D					

11

Environmental Awareness

1. What is the aim of water conservation?

   A. To manage fresh water as a sustainable resource
   B. To increase water pollution
   C. To waste water resources
   D. To desalinate sea water

2. One of the following is NOT a correct way to conserve water domestically?

   A. Ensuring there are no leaks in the house
   B. Using water-efficient flushes
   C. Leaving taps running while brushing teeth
   D. Using appropriate amount of detergent and water for washing clothes

3. How one can minimize evaporation when watering lawns and gardens?

   A. Watering during the hottest part of the day
   B. Watering in the morning or evening
   C. Watering continuously for hours
   D. Not watering at all

4. Which method is used to detect leaks and monitor water usage in a house?

   A. By using a thermometer
   B. By checking the water bill and water meter
   C. By using a metal detector
   D. By checking the electricity bill

5. What should be done with the first set of rainwater in a roof catchment system?

   A. It should be used for drinking
   B. It should be allowed to run to waste
   C. It should be stored immediately
   D. It should be mixed with sewage

6. How energy conservation is achieved?

   A. Increasing energy consumption
   B. Increasing use of renewable energy
   C. Increasing use of non-renewable energy
   D. Increasing use of generators

7. Which of the following is an energy-efficient equipment?

   A. Incandescent bulbs
   B. Conventional heaters
   C. LED lights
   D. Gas-powered generators

8. What is the benefit of using public transport systems?

   A. Reducing the burden of fuel energy
   B. Increasing personal vehicle usage
   C. Increasing traffic congestion
   D. Decreasing public safety

9. Energy derived from sun is known as________.

   A. Wind energy
   B. Nuclear energy
   C. Solar energy
   D. Geothermal energy

10. How biogas is produced?

    A. By burning fossil fuels
    B. By breaking down organic matter anaerobically

C. By extracting it from coal mines
D. By converting solar energy

11. What is the purpose of rainwater harvesting?

A. To accumulate and store rainwater for reuse
B. To increase water pollution
C. To desalinate sea water
D. To increase surface runoff

12. Which of the following is NOT a method/type of rainwater harvesting system?

A. Ground catchment systems
B. Roof catchment systems
C. Subsurface dykes
D. Seawater desalination

13. Subsurface dyke is used for__________.

A. Generating electricity
B. Controlling groundwater flow and increasing groundwater level
C. Building roads
D. Fishing

14. Why is it important to harvest rainwater in urban areas?

A. To increase soil moisture levels
B. To provide supplemental water for city's requirements
C. To mitigate urban flooding
D. All of the above

15. Which irrigation method can save large amount of water in agriculture?

 A. Drip irrigation
 B. Flood irrigation
 C. Sprinkler irrigation
 D. Canal irrigation

16. Which industry practice can save large amounts of water?

 A. Cooling water recirculation
 B. Ignoring water leaks
 C. Using more fresh water
 D. Increasing water waste

17. What is a common method used by water utilities to conserve water?

 A. Ignoring leaks
 B. Leak detection and repairing water lines
 C. Increasing water prices only
 D. Using more water

18. Which is a renewable source of energy?

 A. Coal
 B. Solar energy
 C. Natural gas
 D. Oil

19. Appropriate utilization of ________ can reduce the consumption of electricity in public lighting.

 A. Using CFLs and solar lighting
 B. Leaving lights on all day
 C. Using only incandescent bulbs
 D. Using fossil fuel lamps

20. Which of the following is an energy-efficient building design practice?

    A. Using large glass windows
    B. Proper ventilation and insulation
    C. Building with non-renewable materials
    D. Increasing the number of elevators

21. What should be done to prevent wasteful use of electricity?

    A. Leaving all lights on
    B. Ignoring energy-efficient practices
    C. Using high-wattage bulbs
    D. Switching off lights when not needed

22. What is the role of rainwater harvesting in reducing soil erosion?

    A. Increasing surface runoff
    B. Decreasing groundwater recharge
    C. Preventing surface water runoff during monsoon
    D. None of the above

23. Which source of energy involves converting kinetic energy into electricity?

    A. Solar energy
    B. Wind energy
    C. Biogas
    D. Nuclear energy

24. What is the main environmental benefit of using solar energy?

 A. Increasing air pollution
 B. Producing greenhouse gases
 C. No water and air pollution is generated
 D. Increasing dependency on fossil fuels

1. A	2. C	3. B	4. B	5. B	6. D	7. C	8. A	9. C	10. B
11. A	12. D	13. B	14. D	15. A	16. A	17. B	18. B	19. A	20. B
21. D	22. C	23. B	24.C						

12

Obstacle Training

1. What is the aim/ purpose of obstacle course training for NCC cadets?

   A. To teach navigation skills
   B. To improve communication skills
   C. To develop physical strength and confidence
   D. To learn map reading

2. What material is NOT mentioned as being used for constructing obstacles?

   A. Wood B. Concrete C. Mud D. Steel

3. How far apart are the obstacles typically placed?

   A. 10 feet B. 20 feet C. 30 feet D. 40 feet

4. What is the height of the Straight Balance obstacle above ground level?

   A. 1-foot B. 1 ½ feet C. 2 feet D. 2 ½ feet

5. How long is the Clear Jump obstacle?

   A. 10 feet B. 12 feet C. 18 feet D. 20 feet

6. What is the correct method to successfully cross the Gate Vault?

   A. Crawl under the bars
   B. Jump over both bars
   C. Hold the upper beam and jump across using the lower bar
   D. Walk across carefully

7. What is the length of the Zig-Zag Balance obstacle?

   A. 10 feet   B. 12 feet   C. 15 feet   D. 18 feet

8. How high is the High Wall obstacle?

   A. 4 feet   B. 5 feet   C. 7 feet   D. 6 feet

9. What is the approximate depth of each ditch in the Double Ditch obstacle?

   A. 2-3 feet   B. 3-4 feet   C. 4-5 feet   D. 5-6 feet

10. Which hand is used to support the cadet in the Right-Hand Vault?

    A. Left hand   C. Both hands
    B. Right hand   D. No hands

11. What is 'Ramp obstacle'?

    A. A straight bar
    B. A wooden balance beam
    C. A series of ditches
    D. A sloppy hillock

12. What is the use/benefit of obstacle training?

    A. Developing map reading skills
    B. Ensuring physical fitness and mental strength
    C. Improving culinary skills
    D. Learning to swim

13. Which safety measure is NOT mentioned for obstacle training?

    A. Use of protective gear
    B. Supervision by qualified instructors

C. Training in PT dress
D. Arrangement of first aid

14. Define 'Straight Balance obstacle'.

    A. A series of bars
    B. A concrete wall
    C. A muddy trench
    D. A wooden piece above ground level

15. Which quality is NOT specifically developed through obstacle training?

    A. Flexibility
    B. Culinary skills
    C. Mental strength
    D. Risk-taking ability

16. What is the standard length of the wooden slab in the Straight Balance obstacle?

    A. 10 feet B. 12 feet C. 15 feet D. 18 feet

17. Which obstacle involves jumping across two ditches?

    A. High Wall
    B. Gate Vault
    C. Double Ditch
    D. Ramp

18. For the Right Hand Vault, how high above the ground is the wooden slab?

    A. 2 ½ feet B. 3 feet C. 4 feet D. 3 ½ feet

19. Which obstacle is similar to the Right-Hand Vault but uses the opposite hand?

    A. Clear Jump
    B. Left Hand Vault
    C. Zig-Zag Balance
    D. High Wall

20. In the Gate Vault obstacle, what is the height of the upper bar?

    A. 3 feet B. 4 feet C. 5 feet D. 6 feet

1. C	2. D	3. C	4. B	5. C	6. C	7. D	8. A	9. B	10. B
11. D	12. B	13. A	14. D	15. B	16. B	17. C	18. D	19. B	20. C

SPECIAL SUBJECT
(Army)

01

Armed Forces

1.1 BASIC ORGANISATION OF ARMED FORCES

1. Who is the Supreme Commander of the Indian Armed Forces?

   A. Prime Minister
   B. President of India
   C. Chief of Army Staff
   D. Chief of defence staff

2. Who assists the Chief of Army Staff (COAS)?

   A. Vice Chief of Army Staff
   B. Principle Staff Officers
   C. Deputy Chief of Army Staff
   D. All of the above

3. How many theatre commands does the Indian Army have?

   A. Five B. Six C. Seven D. Eight

4. Which of the following city has headquarter of Northern Command of Indian Army?

   A. Kolkata
   B. Pune
   C. Jaipur
   D. Udhampur

5. Which India Army command is headquartered in Pune?

   A. Eastern Command
   B. Southern Command
   C. Central Command
   D. Western Command

6. What is the primary objective of the Indian Navy?

   A. Protecting land borders
   B. Securing maritime borders
   C. Conducting aerial warfare
   D. Cyber warfare

7. The Indian Navy is commanded by__________.

   A. Vice Chief of Naval Staff
   B. Chief of Naval Staff
   C. Admiral of the Fleet
   D. Commanding Officer

8. Where is the headquarter of the Western Naval Command located?

   A. Vishakhapatnam
   B. Mumbai
   C. Kochi
   D. Chennai

9. How many Navy commands are there Indian?

   A. Three B. Four C. Five D. Six

10. Indian Navy's world's rank in terms of size is________.

    A. Third B. Fourth C. Fifth D. Sixth

11. Indian Air Force established in which year/ come into existence?

    A. 1947 B. 1932 C. 1950 D. 1965

12. Who commands the Indian Air Force?

    A. Chief of Air Operations
    B. Air Chief Marshal
    C. Chief of Defence Staff
    D. Chief of Air Staff

13. Which Indian Air Force command is headquartered in Allahabad/Prayag raj, Uttar Pradesh?

    A. Western Air Command
    B. Southern Air Command
    C. Central Air Command
    D. Eastern Air Command

14. Where is the headquarters of Training Command of Indian Air Force located?

    A. Bangalore, Karnataka
    B. Gandhinagar, Gujarat
    C. Nagpur, Maharashtra
    D. Shillong, Meghalaya

15. How many operational commands does the Indian Air Force have?

    A. Five B. Six C. Seven D. Eight

16. What is the rank of officer who commands the functional commands of Indian Air Force?

    A. Air Chief Marshal
    B. Air Marsha
    C. Air Vice Marshal
    D. Air Officer Commanding-in-Chief

17. Which Indian Air Force command is headquartered in Shillong, Meghalaya?

    A. Eastern Air Command
    B. Southern Air Command
    C. South Western Air Command
    D. Western Air Command

18. Headquarters of Maintenance Command of Indian Air Force located at________.

    A. Bangalore, Karnataka
    B. Nagpur, Maharashtra
    C. Gandhinagar, Gujarat
    D. Shillong, Meghalaya

19. What is the primary responsibility of the Indian Air Force?

    A. Securing maritime borders
    B. Securing Indian airspace
    C. Ground warfare
    D. Cyber security

20. The officer who commands a command headquarters in the Indian Army holds ________ rank.

    A. Major General
    B. Brigadier
    C. Lieutenant General
    D. Colonel

21. Which Indian Army command is headquartered in Jaipur?

    A. Southern Command
    B. Western Command
    C. South Western Command
    D. Central Command

22. How many deputy chiefs of army staff assist the Chief of Army Staff?

    A. One
    B. Two
    C. Three
    D. Four

23. Which among the following is largest component of the Indian Défense Forces?

A. Indian Navy
B. Indian Air Force
C. Indian Army
D. Indian Coast Guard

24. Where is the headquarter of the Indian Army Training Command located?

A. Shimla B. New Delhi C. Lucknow D. Pune

25. Which Indian Navy command is headquartered in Vishakhapatnam?

A. Western Naval Command
B. Southern Naval Command
C. Eastern Naval Command
D. Central Naval Command

26. What is the primary responsibility of the Indian Air Force?

A. Conducting aerial warfare
B. Ground-based operations
C. Securing maritime borders
D. Cyber defence

27. Where is the headquarter of the South Western Air Command located?

A. Gandhinagar, Gujarat
B. Nagpur, Maharashtra
C. Bangalore, Karnataka
D. Shillong, Meghalaya

28. Match the following

Command Name	Headquarters
1. Army Training Command	A. Udhampur
2. Eastern Command	B. Lucknow
3. Headquarters, Indian Army	C. Pune
4. Western Command	D. Chandi mandir
5. Southern Command	E. New Delhi
6. Central Command	F. Kolkata
7. South Western Command	G. Jaipur
8. Northern Command	H. Shimla

A. 1H, 2F, 3E, 4D, 5C, 6B, 7G, 8A
B. 1A, 2G, 3B, 4D, 5C, 6H, 7E, 8F
C. 1A, 2B, 3C, 4D, 5E, 6F, 7G, 8H
D. 1H, 2F, 3E, 4C, 5D, 6G, 7B, 8A

1. B	2. D	3. C	4. D	5. B	6. B	7. B	8. B	9. A	10. C
11. B	12. D	13. C	14. A	15. A	16. D	17. B	18. B	19. B	20. C
21. C	22. B	23. C	24. A	25. C	26. A	27. A	28. A		

1.2 ORGANISATION OF ARMY

1. What is the mission of Indian Army?

A. Conducting aerial warfare
B. Ensuring national security and unity
C. Maritime defence
D. Cyber security

2. Which operation was conducted by the Indian Army in Kashmir against Pakistan?

   A. Operation Pawan
   B. Kashmir Operations 1947-48
   C. Operation Vijay
   D. Indo-Pak War 1971

3. Which war did the Indian Army fight in 1962?

   A. Indo-Pak War 1965
   B. Kargil Conflict
   C. Sino-Indian Operations in NEFA and Ladakh
   D. Sri Lanka Operations

4. Where is the headquarter of the Indian Army located?

   A. Mumbai
   B. Pune
   C. New Delhi
   D. Kolkata

5. What is the rank of the officer who commands a Corps in the Indian Army?

   A. Major General
   B. Brigadier
   C. Colonel
   D. Lieutenant General

6. How many divisions are typically under the command of a Corps?

   A. 1-2 B.3-4 C. 5-6 D. 7-8

7. What is the rank of the officer who commands a Division in the Indian Army?

   A. Lieutenant General
   B. Major General
   C. Brigadier
   D. Colonel

8. __________ is the basic unit of a Brigade.

A. Company
B. Battalion
C. Regiment
D. Squadron

9. What is the primary role of the Infantry battalion in the Indian Army?

A. Aerial warfare
B. Securing maritime borders
C. Close battle and capturing territory
D. Cyber defence

10. Which of the following is known for its mobility and firepower?

A. Infantry
B. Engineers
C. Armoured Corps
D. Signals

11. How many tanks are there in an Armoured Regiment?

A. 30
B. 35
C. 45
D. 50

12. The BMP-I and II vehicles are used by__________.

A. Artillery
B. Mechanised Infantry
C. Engineers
D. Army Air Defence

13. What is the role of Army Medical Corps?

A. Providing communication
B. Operating tanks
C. Offering medical aid and running hospitals
D. Managing logistics

14. Which corps is responsible for construction of bridges and demolition?

A. Armoured Corps
B. Engineers
C. Artillery
D. Signals

15. What is the role of Army Service Corps?

A. Ammunition and clothing
B. Rations, fuel, and transport
C. Communication
D. Anti-aircraft weapons

16. Which corps handles the repair and recovery of equipment?

A. Army Ordnance Corps
B. Signals
C. Corps of Electrical and Mechanical Engineers
D. Army Aviation Corps

17. What is the role of Remount and Veterinary Corps deal with?

A. Medical aid
B. Animal transport and dog units
C. Construction
D. Anti-aircraft defence

18. Which branch deals with discipline and protocol in the Indian Army?

A. Judge Advocate General Branch
B. Army Education Corps
C. Corps of Military Police
D. Intelligence Corps

19. What is the role of the Intelligence Corps?

    A. Repair and recovery
    B. Medical aid
    C. Field intelligence
    D. Physical training

20. Which branch of the Indian Army deals with legal assistance?

    A. Corps of Military Police
    B. Judge Advocate General Branch
    C. Army Education Corps
    D. Intelligence Corps

1. B	2. B	3. C	4. C	5. D	6. B	7. B	8. B	9. C	10. C
11. C	12. B	13. C	14. B	15. B	16. C	17. B	18. C	19. C	20. B

1.3 BADGES OF RANKS

1. Which is the highest rank in the Indian Navy?

    A. Admiral
    B. Rear Admiral
    C. Vice Admiral
    D. Admiral of the Fleet

2. Which rank of air force is equivalent to an army general?

    A. Air Chief Marshal
    B. Air Marshal
    C. Wing Commander
    D. Group Captain

3. Which rank of Indian Army is directly below the army general rank?

    A. Brigadier
    B. Major General
    C. Lieutenant General
    D. Colonel

4. Which rank of navy is equivalent to an army major?

   A. Lieutenant Commander
   B. Captain
   C. Commander
   D. Commodore

5. In recognition of Air Force services, the Government of India gave the rank of "Marshall of the Air Force" highest rank in the air force is given to ________

   A. K.M. Cariappa
   B. S.H.F.J. Manekshaw
   C. Arjan Singh
   D. Karan Singh

6. From the following which rank is higher in the Indian Army?

   A. Captain
   B. Major
   C. Subedar Major
   D. Havildar Major

7. What is the lowest rank of commissioned officers in the Indian Navy?

   A. Sub-Lieutenant
   B. Lieutenant
   C. Commander
   D. Captain

8. Which rank is equivalent to a Lieutenant Colonel in the Indian Air Force?

   A. Wing Commander
   B. Group Captain
   C. Squadron Leader
   D. Flight Lieutenant

9. Which rank in the Indian Army is directly above Brigadier?

   A. Lieutenant Colonel
   B. Colonel
   C. Major General
   D. Captain

10. Who was the first person to be awarded the rank of Field Marshal in India?

    A. K.M. Cariappa
    B. Arjan Singh
    C. S.H.F.J. Manekshaw
    D. Jail Singh

11. Which is the highest non-commissioned officer rank in the Indian Army?

    A. Sergeant
    B. Havildar
    C. Naib Subedar
    D. Subedar Major

12. What is the equivalent rank of a Lieutenant General in the Indian Navy?

    A. Vice Admiral
    B. Commodore
    C. Rear Admiral
    D. Captain

13. Which rank is below the rank of Captain in the Indian Navy?

    A. Lieutenant Commander
    B. Commander
    C. Lieutenant
    D. Sub-Lieutenant

14. Which rank in the Indian Army is equivalent to a Wing Commander in the Indian Air Force?

    A. Major
    B. Lieutenant Colonel
    C. Colonel
    D. Brigadier

15. What is the equivalent rank of a Brigadier in the Indian Navy?

    A. Captain
    B. Commodore
    C. Rear Admiral
    D. Vice Admiral

16. Which rank is directly below Wing Commander in the Indian Air Force?

    A. Group Captain
    B. Squadron Leader
    C. Flight Lieutenant
    D. Flying Officer

17. Who was the Indian Army Chief during the 1971 war against Pakistan?

    A. K.M. Cariappa
    B. Arjan Singh
    C. S.H.F.J. Manekshaw
    D. Karan Singh

18. What is the equivalent rank of a Lieutenant in the Indian Air Force?

    A. Flying Officer
    B. Squadron Leader
    C. Flight Lieutenant
    D. Wing Commander

19. What is the rank of a Sub-Lieutenant equivalent to in the Indian Army?

    A. Captain B. Lieutenant C. Major D. Colonel

1. D	2. A	3. C	4. A	5. C	6. B	7. A	8. A	9. C	10. A
11. D	12. A	13. B	14. B	15. B	16. B	17. C	18. A	19. B	

1.4 TASK AND ROLE OF FIGHTING ARMY

1. Which part of the army is essential for close combat?

    A. Armour
    B. Infantry
    C. Artillery
    D. Engineers

2. What is the primary role of mechanized infantry?

    A. Reconnaissance
    B. Holding ground
    C. Close with and destroy or capture the enemy
    D. Air defence

3. Which of the following is a basic characteristic of an infantry?

   A. High altitude flying
   B. Self-reliance
   C. Naval operations
   D. Electronic warfare

4. What does armour rely on to achieve surprise?

   A. Camouflage
   B. Speed
   C. Air support
   D. Artillery fire

5. Which type of unit can be employed in any operation of war?

   A. Engineers
   B. Artillery
   C. Infantry
   D. Signal Corps

6. What provides protection to mechanized infantry?

   A. Heavy artillery
   B. Air defence systems
   C. Light armour of the armoured personnel carrier
   D. Camouflage nets

7. What is the primary means of communication in a mechanized infantry unit?

   A. Telephone
   B. Radio
   C. Signal flags
   D. Pigeon

8. What is the role of armour in defensive operations?

   A. Digging trenches
   B. Offensive action
   C. Holding ground
   D. Repairing vehicles

9. What is the most important characteristic of infantry?

   A. Mobility
   B. Self-reliance
   C. Speed
   D. Heavy artillery

10. Which characteristic allows mechanized infantry to operate across water obstacles?

A. High speed
B. Amphibious capability
C. Heavy armour
D. Stealth technology

11. What is the basis of all infantry tactics?

A. Artillery support
B. Fire and movement
C. Air support
D. Signal communication

12. Which type of action should be given to armour?

A. Defensive
B. Offensive
C. Reconnaissance
D. Logistic

13. Which unit is best suited for holding ground?

A. Artillery
B. Infantry
C. Engineers
D. Signal Corps

14. Infantry highly adaptable to do which type of operations?

A. Naval operations
B. Space missions
C. Any type of ground operations
D. Cyber warfare

15. What is the shock effect of mechanized infantry?

A. Heavy artillery
B. Stealth
C. Firepower and mobility
D. Electronic warfare

16. What is the primary task of the army during an offensive action?

    A. Building fortifications
    B. Close with and destroy the enemy
    C. Maintain supply lines
    D. Provide medical support

17. Which characteristic of armour allows it to produce decisive results?

    A. Concentration
    B. Light armour
    C. Signal communication
    D. Stealth

18. What type of mobility does infantry have?

    A. High altitude flying
    B. Cross-country
    C. Underwater
    D. Space travel

19. Which type of personnel are armed with carbines and pistols?

    A. Engineers
    B. Signal Corps
    C. Certain infantry personnel
    D. Artillery

20. What is the basic infantry weapon?

    A. Missile
    B. Rifle and bayonet
    C. Tank
    D. Fighter jet

1. B	2. C	3. B	4. B	5. C	6. C	7. B	8. B	9. B	10. B
11. B	12. B	13. B	14. C	15. C	16. B	17. A	18. B	19. C	20. B

1.5 TASK AND ROLE OF SUPPORTING ARMS AND SERVICES

1. What is the primary role of the infantry in the Indian Army?

   A. Conduct aerial reconnaissance
   B. Close in with the enemy and destroy or capture him
   C. Provide logistical support
   D. Secure maritime borders

2. Which characteristic of infantry allows it to operate over any type of ground?

   A. Vulnerability
   B. Adaptability
   C. Self-reliance
   D. Mobility

3. Which of the following is the main vulnerability area of infantry?

   A. Lack of firepower
   B. Ground action, air attack, and anti-personnel mines
   C. Poor communication
   D. Limited mobility

4. Which of the following is not a role of mechanized infantry?

   A. Reconnaissance
   B. Counter infiltration
   C. Maritime defence
   D. Hold ground temporarily

5. What is the role of armour in the Indian Army?

   A. Conduct naval operations
   B. Provide medical aid
   C. Destroy the enemy by mobile and offensive action
   D. Conduct cyber warfare

6. Which principle of armour emphasizes for employment in mass for maximum shock effect?

   A. Flexibility
   B. Concentration
   C. Surprise
   D. Cooperation

7. What is achieved by armour through weight, violence, and direction of attack?

   A. Flexibility
   B. Concentration
   C. Surprise
   D. Cooperation

8. Flexibility of armour depends upon ________

   A. Heavy armour
   B. Good physical mobility and excellent means of command and control
   C. Large number of troops
   D. Advanced weaponry

9. One of the following is not a component of combined battle groups of armour?

   A. Tanks
   B. Mechanized infantry
   C. Artillery
   D. Submarines

10. What is the primary role of artillery in the Indian Army?

    A. Provide air defence
    B. Support infantry and armour with firepower

C. Conduct reconnaissance
D. Provide medical aid

11. Which warfare is used by mechanized infantry?

A. Naval warfare
B. Cyber warfare
C. Mobile warfare
D. Aerial warfare

12. is a characteristic feature of mechanized infantry allowing it to produce a shock effect?

A. Heavy armour
B. Communication
C. Firepower
D. Mobility

13. In mechanized infantry receiving and passing orders quickly is possible because of _________.

A. Written notes
B. Signal flags
C. Radio communication
D. Runners

14. What is the primary task of infantry in defence?

A. Conducting aerial strikes
B. Holding ground against all forms of attacks
C. Securing maritime borders
D. Conducting cyber operations

15. In infantry tactics, what does the term 'fire and movement' refers to _________

A. Coordinated aerial attacks
B. Moving while simultaneously providing fire support
C. Conducting naval operations
D. Static defence strategy

16. What is the role of the engineer corps in the Indian Army?

    A. Conduct aerial reconnaissance
    B. Build and demolish bridges
    C. Provide medical aid
    D. Conduct cyber defence

17. Which characteristic feature of the infantry allows it to operate under any climatic conditions?

    A. Vulnerability
    B. Mobility
    C. Adaptability
    D. Self-reliance

1. B	2. B	3. B	4. C	5. B	6. B	7. C	8. B	9. D	10. B
11. C	12. C	13. C	14. B	15. B	16. B	17. C			

1.6 HONOURS AND AWARDS

1. The highest military gallantry award in India is______.

   A. Maha Vir Chakra (MVC)
   B. Param Vir Chakra (PVC)
   C. Ashoka Chakra (AC)
   D. Vir Chakra (VC)

2. Which award is given for distinguished service during peacetime?

   A. Param Vir Chakra
   B. Shaurya Chakra(SC)
   C. Param Vishisht Seva Medal (PVSM)
   D. Sena Medal (SM)

3. Nao Sena Medal is given in recognize of _________.

   A. Gallantry in war
   B. Gallantry in peace

C. Distinguished service in the Navy
D. Distinguished service in army and navy

4. Which of the following is a peacetime gallantry award?

A. Ashoka Chakra
B. Maha Vir Chakra
C. Vir Chakra
D. Param Vir Chakra

5. Chiefs of Staff Commendation Card awarded for?

A. Gallantry in the face of the enemy
B. Gallantry other than in the face of the enemy
C. Distinguished service
D. Peacetime bravery

6. Which award is given specifically for bravery in the Air Force?

A. Sena Medal
B. Nao Sena Medal
C. Vayu Sena Medal
D. Shaurya Chakra

7. Which of the following awards is not a gallantry award?

A. Param Vir Chakra
B. Maha Vir Chakra
C. Uttam Yudh Seva Medal (UYSM)
D. Vir Chakra

8. Which medal is awarded for distinguished service during wartime?

A. Param Vishisht Seva Medal
B. Sarvottam Yudh Seva Medal (SYSM)
C. Shaurya Chakra
D. Sena Medal

9. The Kirti Chakra award is given under which category?

   A. Gallantry in the face of enemy
   B. Peacetime gallantry
   C. Distinguished service in war
   D. Distinguished service in peace

10. Which award is higher in precedence, the Vir Chakra or the Maha Vir Chakra?

   A. Vir Chakra
   B. Maha Vir Chakra
   C. Both are the same
   D. Depends on the context

11. Which award is given for exceptional service in the Indian Army, Navy, and Air Force during peacetime?

   A. Sena Medal
   B. Nao Sena Medal
   C. Vayu Sena Medal
   D. Vishisht Seva Medal (VSM)

12. Which of the following is not a wartime gallantry award?

   A. Param Vir Chakra
   B. Maha Vir Chakra
   C. Vir Chakra
   D. Ashoka Chakra

13. Which award is given for acts of gallantry in the face of enemy?

   A. Kirti Chakra
   B. Shaurya Chakra
   C. Param Vir Chakra
   D. Ati Vishisht Seva Medal

14. Which award is equivalent to the Sena Medal but specifically for the Air Force?

A. Param Vir Chakra
B. Kirti Chakra
C. Vayu Sena Medal
D. Shaurya Chakra

15. Which of the following is a Gallantry Award for wartime bravery?

A. Sarvottam Yudh Seva Medal
B. Ashoka Chakra
C. Param Vir Chakra
D. Vishisht Seva Medal

16. Which award is given for Gallantry other than in the face of the enemy (Peace Time)?

A. Maha Vir Chakra
B. Kirti Chakra
C. Vir Chakra
D. Param Vishisht Seva Medal

17. Sena Medal can be awarded during _________.

A. Wartime only
B. Peacetime only
C. Both wartime and peacetime
D. Distinguished service only

18. Which of the following is not a Gallantry Award?

A. Vir Chakra
B. Nao Sena Medal
C. Ati Vishisht Seva Medal
D. Vayu Sena Medal

19. The Chief of Staff Commendation Card is awarded for:

    A. Wartime bravery
    B. Distinguished service
    C. Peacetime bravery
    D. All of the above

20. Which medal is awarded for distinguished service of a high order during peacetime?

    A. Kirti Chakra
    B. Maha Vir Chakra
    C. Param Vishisht Seva Medal
    D. Vir Chakra

21. The Ashoka Chakra is awarded for

    A. Gallantry in the face of the enemy
    B. Gallantry other than in the face of the enemy
    C. Distinguished service
    D. Wartime bravery

22. Which of the following is a Non-Gallantry Award?

    A. Sena Medal
    B. Vishisht Seva Medal
    C. Vir Chakra
    D. Kirti Chakra

23. The Nao Sena Medal is awarded to personnel of which service?

    A. Army
    B. Navy
    C. Air Force
    D. All of the above

24. The Shaurya Chakra is given for:

    A. Distinguished service
    B. Wartime bravery
    C. Peacetime gallantry
    D. Both wartime and peacetime bravery

25. Which award is higher in precedence: Maha Vir Chakra or Vir Chakra?

A. Maha Vir Chakra
B. Both are equal
C. Vir Chakra
D. None of the above

26. Which medal is given for service during war or conflict situations?

A. Sarvottam Yudh Seva Medal
B. Kirti Chakra
C. Param Vishisht Seva Medal
D. Vayu Sena Medal

27. The Vishisht Seva Medal is awarded for:

A. Gallantry in the face of the enemy
B. Gallantry other than in the face of the enemy
C. Distinguished service
D. Wartime bravery

28. The highest peace time gallantry award is_________.

A. Shaurya Chakra
B. Sena Medal
C. Kirti Chakra
D. Ashoka Chakra

29. Who can receive the Sena Medal?

A. Only Army personnel
B. Army, Navy, and Air Force personnel
C. Only Navy personnel
D. Only Air Force personnel

30. The Uttam Yudh Seva Medal is given for _________.

    A. Peace time distinguished service
    B. Peacetime bravery
    C. Gallantry in the face of the enemy
    D. Wartime distinguished service

31. The Param Vishisht Seva Medal is awarded for_________.

    A. Exceptional courage
    B. Distinguished service of the highest order
    C. Gallantry during wartime
    D. Gallantry during peacetime

1. A	2. C	3. C	4. A	5. B	6. C	7. C	8. B	9. B	10. B
11. D	12. D	13. C	14. C	15. C	16. B	17. C	18. C	19. D	20. C
21. B	22. B	23. B	24. C	25. A	26. A	27. C	28. D	29. B	30. D
31. B									

02

Map Reading

2.1 INTRODUCTION TO MAPS AND CONVENTIONAL SIGNS

1. What is the definition of a map?

   A. A representation of selected natural and manmade features of the entire earth's surface on a sheet of paper
   B. A representation of selected natural features only
   C. A representation of selected manmade features only
   D. A representation of the entire earth's surface without any scale or correct geographical positions

2. What is map?

   A. Map is the geographical representation of land on a paper
   B. Map is demography of a country
   C. Map is choice of signs on paper
   D. Map is universally accepted paper

3. Which of the following is NOT a characteristic of a map?

   A. Definite scale
   B. Correct relative geographical positions and elevations
   C. Random placement of features
   D. Use of symbols, color differences, and contours

4. What do symbols, color differences, and contours on a map help to show?

   A. Political boundaries
   B. Population density
   C. Physical features such as mountains, valleys, and plains
   D. Weather patterns

5. Who prepares and publishes maps in India?

   A. National Weather Service
   B. National Mapping Organization
   C. International Cartography Association
   D. United Nations Development Programme

6. What is the science of making maps called?

   A. Geography
   B. Geology
   C. Cartography
   D. Meteorology

7. Which organization prepares topographical maps in India?

   A. National Geographic Society
   B. Geological Survey of India
   C. Survey of India
   D. Indian Cartographic Society

8. What is one limitation of a map?

   A. Lack of color differentiation
   B. Lack of symbols
   C. Lack of a definite scale
   D. Inability to represent the entire earth's surface

9. What is Altals Map? Or Which of the following best describes Atlas Maps?

   A. Detailed maps focusing on specific regions or cities
   B. Maps showing the entire world or large regions on a single sheet
   C. Maps providing detailed information about topography and terrain
   D. Maps exclusively depicting political boundaries and borders of countries

10. Survey of India maps are __________ .

   A. Political maps highlighting administrative boundaries
   B. Weather maps showing atmospheric conditions
   C. Topographical maps focusing on terrain features and elevation
   D. Geological maps illustrating the composition of the Earth's crust

11. Which of the following statements accurately describes Relief Maps?

   A. Relief Maps are virtual maps displayed on computer screens
   B. Relief Maps are maps primarily used for navigating through cities
   C. Relief Maps are three-dimensional models representing terrain features
   D. Relief Maps are maps specifically designed for maritime navigation

12. Which type of map provides information about winds, atmospheric pressures, and other atmospheric conditions?

    A. Topographic map
    C. Statistical
    B. Meteorological
    D. Geological map

13. Which of the following maps shows information of population, industries, mineral ores, crops etc.

    A. Topographic map
    C. Statistical
    B. Meteorological
    D. Geological map

14. Conventional signs are symbols used for representing on a map?

    A. Representing natural features
    B. Identifying geographic coordinates
    C. Depicting weather patterns
    D. Artificial or natural features/objects

15. Identify the conventional signs for the mentioned numbers

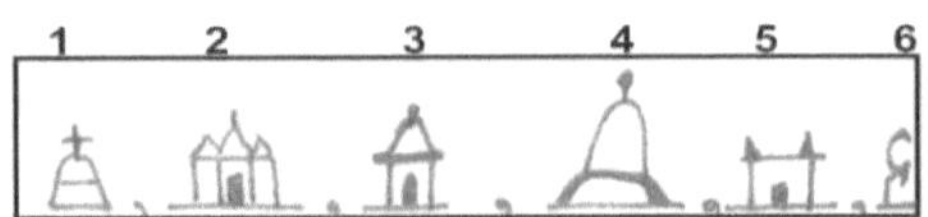

    A. 1. Tomb, 2. Temple, 3. Pagoda, 4. Mosque, 5. Church, 6. Idgah
    B. 1. Church, 2. Mosque, 3. Temple, 4. Pagoda, 5. Idgah, 6. Tomb
    C. 1. Temple, 2. Mosque, 3. Church, 4. Tomb, 5. Idgah, 6. Pagoda
    D. 1. Church, 2. Temple 3. Mosque, 4. Idgah, 5. Pagoda, 6. Tomb

16. Identify the conventional sign used for

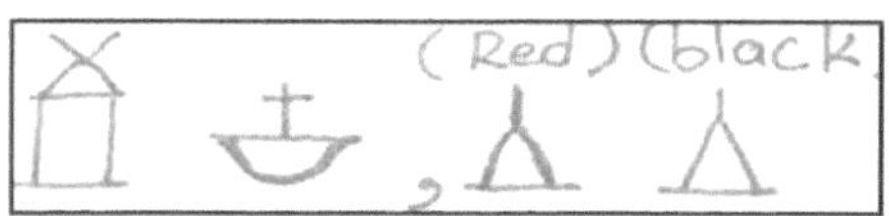

A. Light house-light ship C. Ship/Boat
B. Tom D. Fort and huts

17. Identify the conventional signs for the mentioned numbers

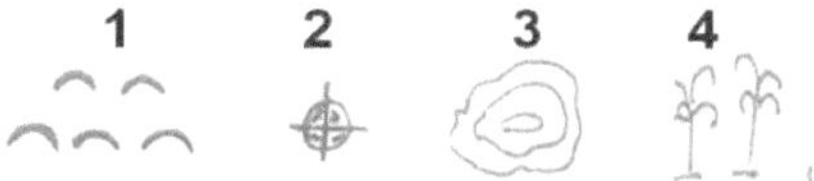

A. 1. Graves, 2. Oil wells, 3. Contours, 4. Palms
B. 1. Sand dunes, 2. well, 3. Spring, 4. Palms
C. 1. Village, 2. Pipeline, 3. Lake, 4. Palms
D. 1. Graves, 2. Tube wells, 3. Contours, 4. Palms

18. Identify the conventional signs for the mentioned numbers

A. 1. Cart, camel and mule path, 2 Footpath, 3. road in bed of stream, 4. Level crossing
B. 1. Village road, 2. Telephone line, 3. Curved road, 4. Railway track
C. 1. Mountain terrain, 2 Telephone line, 3. canal, 4. Railway line
D. 1. Cart track, 2. Electricity line, 3. Curved road, 4. Over bridge

19. Which of the following is a broken ground?

20. Below conventional sign represents

A. Bridges with pier sand without, Causeway, Ford
B. Embankments, road or rail, tank cutting tunnel
C. Railways, broad-gauge, Double, Single (Station), under construction
D. Stream-approx, water course, canal

1. A	2. A	3. C	4. C	5. B	6. C	7. C	8. C	9. B	10. C
11. C	12. B	13. C	14. A	15. B	16. A	17. A	18. A	19. A	20. A

2.2 SCALE AND GRID SYSTEMS

1. What is the purpose of scales on maps?

A. They help to determine the shapes of objects on map
B. They assist in calculating distances from one place to another
C. They indicate the map's publication date
D. They show the map's elevation levels

2. How does the area covered by a map relate to its scale?

A. The smaller the area covered, the smaller the scale.
B. The larger the area covered, the smaller the scale

C. The smaller the area covered, the larger the scale
D. There is no relationship between the area covered and the scale

3. If two maps are of the same size but one has a scale of 1:50,000 and the other has a scale of 1:25,000, how does the area covered by the first map compare to the second?

   A. It covers half the area covered by the second map
   B. It covers twice the area covered by the second map
   C. It covers four times the area covered by the second map
   D. It covers one-fourth the area of the second map

4. What information does every map carry besides the scale?

   A. Topographic features
   B. The map's date of creation
   C. Political boundaries
   D. A depiction of the scale

5. What does a scale of 1:50,000 indicate on a map?

   A. One unit on the map represents 50,000 units in reality
   B. One unit in reality represents 50,000 units on the map
   C. The map covers an area of 50,000 square units
   D. The map's dimensions are 50,000 units by 50,000 units

6. Scale represents __________

   A. Proportion of two points on map and two points on the ground
   B. Proportion of several points on map and several points on the ground
   C. Proportion of two lines on map and two lines on the ground
   D. Proportion of one point on map and one point on the ground

7. Which of the following statements accurately describe methods of expressing a scale?

   A. In Words: The scale is expressed using numerical ratios, indicating the relationship between measurements on the map and the corresponding measurements on the ground.
   B. As a Representative Fraction (RF): The scale is represented as a fraction, where the numerator signifies the unit on the map and the denominator signifies the same unit on the ground.
   C. Both (A) and (B)
   D. Neither (A) nor (B)

8. In map scale of "1 inch to 1 mile," what does it mean?

   A. One inch on the map represents one mile on the ground
   B. One mile on the map represents one inch on the ground
   C. One inch on the map represents one centimeter on the ground
   D. One mile on the map represents one foot on the ground

9. How is the scale expressed in the method of a Representative Fraction (RF)?

   A. In words
   B. In numerical ratios
   C. As a fraction
   D. Markings

10. If the scale of a map is given as 1/100000, what does it signify?

    A. One unit on the map represents 100,000 units on the ground
    B. One unit on the ground represents 100,000 units on the map
    C. One inch on the map represents 100,000 inches on the ground
    D. One centimeter on the map represents 100,000 centimeters on the ground

11. What is Grid? Or Define Grid?

    A. A systematic pattern of vertical and horizontal imaginary lines drawn on Earth
    B. A pattern of vertical and zig-zag horizontal lines drawn on Earth
    C. Connecting lines between north pole and south pose
    D. Connecting lines between several cardinal points of earth

12. Which of the following is grid lines?

    A. Lines running parallel to earth surface
    B. Lines running horizontal to earth surface
    C. Zig-zag lines running on earth surface
    D. Both parallel and horizontal lines running on earth surface

13. What do we call the combinations of vertical and horizontal lines on Earth's systematic pattern?

A. Latitude and Longitude
B. Grid Lines
C. Equator
D. Tropics

14. Which line divides Earth into the Northern and Southern Hemispheres?

A. Latitude
B. Longitude
C. Grid Lines
D. Equator

15. Which line divides Earth into the Eastern and Western Hemispheres?

A. Latitude
B. Longitude
C. Grid Lines
D. Equator

16. What is the purpose of Grid Lines on Earth's systematic pattern?

A. To mark the Equator
B. To measure distances between continents
C. To measure bearings and reading Grid References
D. To track the movement of tectonic plates

17. Easting lines and northing lines are ________ coloured vertical lines and horizontal lines?

A. Black
B. Red
C. Pink
D. Brown

18. Which of the following statement is true for giving a Grid Reference?

1. Grid references can be of 4, 6, 8 and 10 figures
2. To get grid reference always count Easting lines from west to east and Northing lines from south to north

3. Most commonly six figure grid reference is used
4. To get grid reference always count Northing lines from south to north and then Easting lines from west to east

A. All are true
B. 1, 2 and 3 are true
C. 1, 3 and 4 are true
D. 4. Only 4 is true

19. Find the grid reference of 'A'

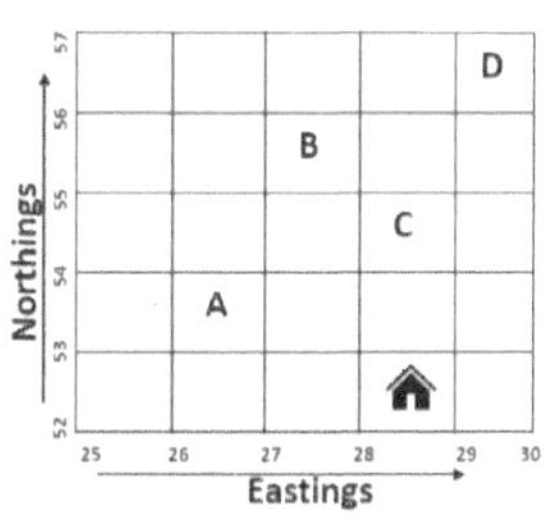

A. 2653
B. 2654
C. 2754
D. 26275354

20. Find the grid reference of 'D'.

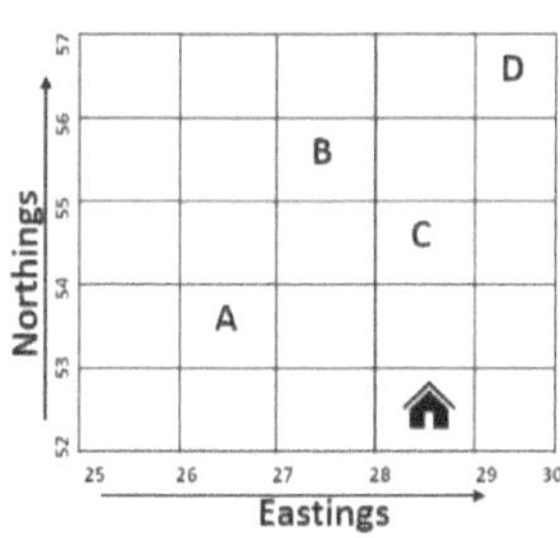

A. 3057
B. 2956
C. 2957
D. 29305657

21. Find the grid reference of 'The House'.

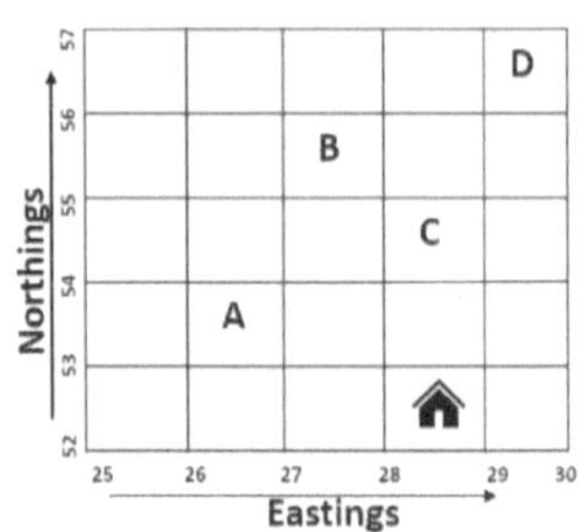

A. 2953
B. 2953
C. 2852
D. 29285253

22. Find the 6-figure grid reference of 'Triangle'.

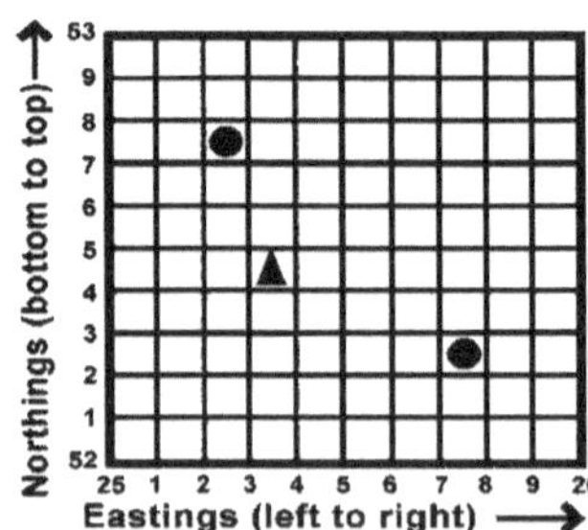

A. 253524
B. 254524
C. 253525
D. 255234

23. Which of the following skills are essential for effective and correct map reading?
    1. Identifying different types of terrain
    2. Memorizing geographical landmarks
    3. Differentiating between maps of different scales
    4. Recognizing weather patterns depicted on the map

5. Finding the correct Grid Reference of objects
6. Calculating the elevation of mountains

A. All C. None of them
B. Only 3 and 5 D. Only 4, 5 and 6

24. Bearing is always measured in ________

A. Clock wise C. Both A and B
B. Counter clock wise D. None of these

1. B	2. A	3. C	4. D	5. B	6. A	7. C	8. A	9. C	10. A
11. A	12. D	13. B	14. D	15. B	16. C	17. A	18. B	19. A	20. B
21. C	22. A	23. B	24						

2.3 TOPOGRAPHICAL FORMS AND TECHNICAL TERMS

1. Any feature whether natural or artificial which could cause a body of troops to contract its front is known as________.

A. Spur B. Saddle C. Knoll D. Defile

2. A small isolated hill is known as ________

A. Spur B. Saddle C. Knoll D. Defile

3. A narrow ridge of high land joining up to higher hills is known as

A. Col or saddle C. Knoll
B. Defile D. Saddle

4. What is dead ground?

   A. Ground which is because of undulations or hills is not visible to the observer's eye
   B. Ground which is flat found over the hills and not visible to the observer
   C. Ground which is hidden from under the water
   D. Ground without any vegetation cover

5. __________ is that line on the range of hills or mountains from which the ground slopes down in opposite direction.

   A. Spur
   B. Crest
   C. Plateau
   D. Escarpment

6. A line drawn on the map joining up all points of equal height above sea level is called as?

   A. Contours
   B. Grid line
   C. Spot height
   D. Horizontal angle

7. The difference between True North and Magnetic North is __________

   A. Magnetic angle
   B. Magnetic radiance
   C. Magnetic variance
   D. None

1. D	2. C	3. A	4. A	5. B	6. A	7. C

2.4 RELIEF, CONTOURS AND GRADIENTS

1. Which one of the following is the definition of relief?

   A. The shape of the ground in a vertical plane
   B. The shape of the ground in a horizontal plane

C. The shape of the ground in a circular plane
D. The shape of the ground in a zig-zag plane

2. The slopes are categorized into two types, convex and concave. Which of the following correctly describes these terms?

   A. A convex slope curves inward, while a concave slope bulges outward
   B. A convex slope bulges outward, while a concave slope curve inward
   C. Both convex and concave slopes bulge outward
   D. Both convex and concave slopes curve inward

3. Contour lines on a map indicates _________

   A. Changes in temperature
   B. Changes in elevation relative to mean sea level
   C. Changes in political boundaries.
   D. Changes in vegetation types

4. Which of the following statements describe characteristics of contour lines on a map?
   1. Contours accurately show height, shape, and slope of the ground.
   2. Contours are typically depicted in brown.
   3. Height is marked on every fifth contour line.
   4. Contour lines exhibit consistent appearance.
   5. Contour lines do not intersect or cross each other. Which statements are true?

   A. 1, 2, 3, and 5
   B. 2, 3, and 5
   C. 1, 2,4 and 5
   D. 1, 4, and 5

5. Which of the following statements accurately defines the vertical interval (VI)?

   A. The distance between two mountain peaks
   B. The distance between two rivers on a topographic map
   C. The rise between successive contour lines on a map
   D. The elevation of a specific landmark above sea level

6. What does the term "horizontal equivalent (HE)" refer to in cartography?

   A. The distance between two peaks on a mountain range
   B. The distance measured along a straight line between two points on a map
   C. The distance measured flat on the map between adjacent contour lines
   D. The horizontal distance between two rivers on a topographic map

7. What is the definition of bearing in navigation?

   A. The distance between two landmarks on a map
   B. The clockwise angle formed by a straight line joining two points and the direction of the North
   C. The elevation of a specific landmark above sea level
   D. The angle formed by a mountain peak and the horizon

8. What is the purpose of the Service Protractor "A" Mark IV in navigation?

   A. It measures distances between two points on a map
   B. It calculates elevations of landmarks above sea level
   C. It plots and measures bearings on a map
   D. It determines the speed of a vessel on the sea

9. Bench Mark: A permanent mark usually cut into a wall to represent _________ for future reference.

   A. Exact height
   B. Exact length
   C. Exact depth
   D. Exact latitude

10. What is gradient?

   A. Height of a hill
   B. Top of a hill
   C. Gradient of a hill
   D. None of these

11. "Vertical Interval (VI)" refers to _________ on a map?

   A. The horizontal distance between two points.
   B. The rise between successive contour lines.
   C. The total elevation of a hill.
   D. The map scale representation.

1. A	2. B	3. B	4. A	5. C	6. C	7. B	8. C	9. A	10. D
11. B									

2.5 CARDINAL POINTS AND TYPES OF NORTH

1. What are the cardinal points?

   A. North, South, East, West
   B. Up, Down, Left, Right
   C. Northeast, Southeast, Southwest, Northwest
   D. None of the above

2. If North is considered as 0 degrees in a standard compass rose, what angle does East form?

   A. 45 degrees
   B. 90 degrees
   C. 180 degrees
   D. 270 degrees

3. Which cardinal point is directly opposite to North?

   A. South
   B. East
   C. West
   D. Northeast

4. Match the following

Cardinal points	Degrees
1. North North East	A. 22 & ½ Degrees
2. East North East	B. 67 & ½ Degrees
3. East South East	C. 112 & ½ Degrees
4. South South East	D. 157 & ½ Degrees
5. South South West	E. 202 & ½ Degrees
6. West South West	F. 247 & ½ Degrees
7. West North West	G. 292 & ½ Degrees
8. North North West	H. 337 & ½ Degrees

   A. 1A, 2B, 3C, 4D, 5E, 6F, 7G, 8H
   B. 1B, 2D, 3C, 4E, 5H, 6F, 7B, 8A

C. 1H, 2G, 3F, 4E, 5D, 6C, 7B, 8A
D. 1C, 2H, 3F, 4G, 5A, 6B, 7D, 8E

5. South south west indicates __________ degrees

A. 202 & ½ Degrees
B. 157 & ½ Degrees
C. 292 & ½ Degrees
D. 90&½ degrees

6. East North East__________indicates __________degrees

A. 202 & ½ Degrees
B. 157 & ½ Degrees
C. 67 & ½ Degrees
D. 90&½ degrees

7. There are __________ types of North?

A. Three B. One C. Two D. Four

8. Match the following

Types of North	Description
1. True North	A. North as per the Grid on map.
2. Magnetic North	B. Point to which the compass needle points
3. Grid North	C. The direction of North Pole from the observer.
4. Magnetic Variation	D. Difference between True North and Magnetic North

A. 1D, 2C, 3B, 4A
B. 1C, 2B, 3A, 4D
C. 1B, 2A, 3C, 4D
D. 1A, 2B, 3C, 4D

9. What is Grid convergence?

A. The angular difference between Grid and True North is called the Angle of Convergence or the Grid Convergence

B. The angular difference between Magnetic and True North is called the Angle of Convergence or the Grid Convergence

C. The angular difference between Grid and Magnetic North is called the Angle of Convergence or the Grid Convergence

D. The angular convergence of Grid, magnetic and true North is called the Angle of Convergence or the Grid Convergence

10. Which factors affect magnetic variation?

A. Pressure and temperature

B. Time and Place

C. Gravity and Time

D. Place and temperature

1. A	2. B	3. A	4. A	5. A	6. C	7. A	8. B	9. A	10. B

2.6 TYPES OF BEARING AND USE OF SERVICE PROTRACTOR

1. There are __________ types of bearing?

A. Three B. One C. Two D. Four

2. Match the following

Types of North	Description
1. Grid Bearing	A. North as per the Grid on map.
2. Magnetic Bearing	B. Measured from Magnetic North by the compass.
3. True Bearing	C. Calculated by finding out the relation of True NORTH and Grid NORTH or Magnetic NORTH

A. 1D, 2C, 3B
B. 1C, 2B, 3A
C. 1B, 2A, 3C
D. 1A, 2B, 3C

3. __________ is an essential link between the compass and the map.

A. Service protractor
B. Divider
C. Indicator
D. Angler

4. Service protractor "A" Mark IV is used for__________?

A. Measuring the distance between two points on a map.
B. Calculating the elevation of a terrain.
C. Measure angles and bearings on the map.
D. Determining the scale of the map.

5. What is the dimensions of a protractor used for mapping and measurement?

A. 8 inches long and 3 inches wide.
B. 5 inches long and 2.5 inches wide
C. 4 inches long and 1 inch wide.
D. 6 inches long and 2 inches wide.

6. Service protractor is made up of which of the following materials?

   A. Made of metal
   B. Made of plastic
   C. Made of cardboard or ivories
   D. Made of glass

7. Prismatic compass is of ________ types

   A. 2 B. 3 C. 4 D. 1

8. Prismatic compass can be of ________ and ________

   A. Solid and dry
   B. Semi solid and fluid
   C. Liquid and dry
   D. Semi dry and semi liquid

9. Deviation of the magnetic needle in a compass from the magnetic NORTH due to impurities or other reasons is known as?

   A. Magnetic declination
   B. Magnetic variation
   C. Compass deviation
   D. Compass error

10. What is the Global Positioning System (GPS)?

   A. A network of weather satellites used for forecasting
   B. A system of satellites and receivers that allows precise location on Earth
   C. A communication system for mobile phones
   D. A series of man-made structures used for navigation

11. The magnetic compass extensively used in__________

    A. For measuring distances on maps D. For predicting weather patterns
    B. For timekeeping in mechanical clocks
    C. In ships, aircraft, and various branches of the army to find & maintain direction

12. When is a map said to be set or oriented?

    A. When it is folded correctly.
    B. When true NORTH on the map pointing to true NORTH on the ground.
    C. When it is used to measure distances accurately.
    D. When it is drawn to scale.

1. A	2. D	3. A	4. C	5. D	6. C	7. A	8. C	9. D	10. B
11. C	12. B								

03

Field Craft and Battle Craft

1. Field craft is an art of _________

   A. Using of ground and the weapon
   B. Using of mines and traps
   C. Using of space and the tactics
   D. Using of aircrafts

2. Which of the following is NOT a subject included in Field Craft?

   A. Visual Training
   B. Judging Distance
   C. Section Formations
   D. Personal Camouflage and Concealment

3. Battle craft is _________

   A. A set of battle drills
   B. A set of ambush
   C. A set of parade drill
   D. A set of commands required in battle

4. What is the purpose of Battle Craft?

   A. To provide heavy firepower in battle
   B. To perform successful operations through essential drills
   C. To establish communication lines
   D. To hold ground in defensive operations

5. Battle craft ensures__________

   A. Physical fitness
   B. Rapid action and avoid confusion
   C. Communication skills
   D. Leadership qualities

6. Which of the following subjects is NOT included in Battle Craft?

   A. Fire and move
   B. Personal camouflage and concealment
   C. Fire control orders
   D. Section battle drills

7. Match the following

Army tactics	Subjects
1. Field craft 2. Battle craft	a. Visual Training.
	b. Section Formations
	c. Movement with and without arms.
	d. Fire discipline and control.
	e. Field Signals.
	f. Fire control orders.
	g. Judging distance
	h. Personal camouflage and concealment.
	i. Fire and move.

   A. 1b, e, g, i; 2a, c, d, f, h
   B. 1a, c, d, g, h; 2b, e, f, i
   C. 1a, b, c, d, e; 2 f, g, h, i
   D. 1 a, c, d, h; 2 b, e, f, g, i

8. What is Battle Craft primarily concerned with?

   A. Strategies for large-scale battles
   B. Set of drills for successful battlefield operations
   C. Logistics and supply chain management
   D. Engineering and construction in military contexts

9. Why are battle drills important?

   A. They ensure effective communication
   B. They save time, ensure rapid action, and avoid confusion
   C. They help in understanding enemy strategies
   D. They improve physical fitness

10. What is essential for the execution of various battle drills?

    A. Advanced weaponry
    B. Knowledge of field signals and section and platoon formations
    C. Detailed maps of the battlefield
    D. High morale

11. What does Field Craft emphasize?

    A. The art of using ground and weapons to one's advantage
    B. Advanced technological warfare
    C. Building fortifications
    D. Navigational skills

12. What is included in Visual Training under Field Craft?

    A. Physical conditioning
    B. Enhancing visual acuity and observation skills

C. Communication skills
D. Tactical planning

13. Which method is used for "Judging distance by noting the detailed appearance of man at various ranges"?

A. Unit of Measure
B. Key Range
C. Appearance Method
D. Section Average

14. Which of the following is a 'Key Range' method of judging distance?

A. Using a known distance to estimate the distance to other objects
B. Using the average distance estimated by the section
C. Halving the distance to an intermediate object and doubling it
D. Bracketing the object between known distances

15. Which of the following subjects of Field Craft deals with the ability to estimate distances visually?

A. Personal Camouflage and Concealment
B. Visual Training
C. Judging Distance
D. Movement with and without Arms

1. A	2. C	3. A	4. B	5. B	6. B	7. B	8. B	9. B	10. B
11. A	12. B	13. C	14. A	15. C					

3.1 JUDGING DISTANCE

1. What is the "Unit of Measure" method in judging distance?

   A. Using a fixed unit like 100 yards
   B. Averaging the estimates of a section
   C. Estimating by appearance
   D. Doubling the distance to a halfway object

2. Which method involves "Estimating the distance to a halfway point and then doubling it"?

   A. Key Range
   B. Halving
   C. Bracketing
   D. Section Average

3. What is the Appearance Method in judging distance?

   A. Using a measuring tape
   B. Judging distance based on the appearance of objects at various ranges
   C. Asking a superior officer
   D. Using a laser rangefinder

4. What is the key principle behind the Halving method of judging distance?

   A. Estimating the distance to an object and dividing it by two
   B. Selecting an object halfway to the target and doubling the distance
   C. Averaging distances estimated by the whole section
   D. Measuring the distance to a nearby landmark

5. Which condition generally causes overestimation of distances?

   A. Bright sunlight
   B. Dead ground between observer and target
   C. Looking through a narrow lane
   D. Large objects

6. What does personal camouflage and concealment entail?

   A. Hiding in bunkers
   B. Using natural and artificial materials to blend in with surroundings
   C. Wearing heavy armor
   D. Setting up decoy positions

7. What is a critical skill included in Judging Distance?

   A. Identifying enemy ranks
   B. Estimating the distance to targets accurately
   C. Communicating under fire
   D. Navigating using a compass

8. Which method of judging distance uses a known measurement, like 100 yards, as a reference?

   A. Appearance Method
   B. Unit of Measure
   C. Key Range
   D. Bracketing

9. What is a "Key Range" method in judging distance?

   A. Estimating based on known distances to certain objects
   B. Using a fixed unit like 100 yards
   C. Halving the distance
   D. Averaging estimates of a section

10. What factor can lead to underestimation of distances?

A. Bad light
B. Small objects
C. Looking uphill
D. Sun in observer's eye

11. What conditions can cause distances to be overestimated during the day?

A. Bright sunlight from behind the observer
B. Small objects in relation to their surroundings
C. Poor lighting and looking through narrow lanes
D. Large objects in relation to their surroundings

12. Judging distance is of how many types?

A. 5 B. 4 C. 7 D. 6

13. Match the following

Method of Judging Distance	Procedure followed
a. Unit of measure	1. The range of the certain object is known, distance to other objects can be found in relation to the known range.
b. Appearance method	2. The average of the answers given by the whole section
c. Section average	3. An object is selected half way between the observer and the target
d. Key range	4. 100 yards method
e. Halving	5. Detailed appearance of man at various ranges

f. Bracketing	6. Maximum and the minimum possible distances of the object and then accepts the mean as the distance.

A. a1, b2, c3, d4, e5, f6
B. a4, b5, c2, d1, e3, f6
C. a3, b4, c1, d2, e5, f6
D. a3, b5, c2, d1, e4, f6

1. A	2. B	3. B	4. B	5. C	6. B	7. B	8. B	9. A	10. C
11. C	12. D	13. B							

3.2 DESCRIPTION OF GROUND

1. Which type of ground is described as "Having little cover and being unsuitable for infantry movement during day?

   A. Broken Ground
   B. Dead Ground
   C. High Ground
   D. Flat and Open Ground

2. A "Dead Ground" refer to__________.

   A. Ground that is above the general level of the area
   B. Ground that is hidden from an observer's view
   C. Ground with little cover
   D. Uneven ground scattered with nullahs

3. In the procedure of describing ground, "Middle Distance" falls under which range?

   A. Up to 300 yards
   B. 300 to 500 yards
   C. Beyond 500 yards
   D. 1000 yards

4. __________ ground is characterized by being uneven and scattered with nullahs and bumps?

   A. Flat and Open Ground
   B. High Ground
   C. Dead Ground
   D. Broken Ground

5. What is the main advantage of high ground in military operations?

   A. It provides natural resources
   B. It facilitates control by observation or fire.
   C. It is easy to traverse
   D. It offers protection from air attacks.

6. Which ground type does not provide cover from high path weapons?

   A. Broken Ground
   B. Dead Ground
   C. Flat and Open Ground
   D. High Ground

7. In the procedure of describing ground, what is the range of the 'Fore Ground' is?

   A. Up to 200 yards
   B. Up to 300 yards
   C. Up to 500 yards
   D. Up to 1000 yards

8. As per the distance, which of the following is correct for describing ground?

   A. Near, Middle, Far
   B. Front, Centre, Rear
   C. Fore Ground, Middle Distance, Distance
   D. Immediate, Intermediate, Extended

9. What is the first step in indicating landmarks using the General Line of Direction (GLD)?

   A. Give left and right boundaries
   B. Point out a centrally located prominent landmark
   C. Describe the ground from left to right
   D. Divide the ground into foreground, middle, and distance

10. When describing the ground, in what direction should you proceed?

   A. From right to left
   B. From front to back
   C. From left to right
   D. From back to front

11. Why is studying and appreciating the ground considered important in military operations?

   A. It helps in resource allocation.
   B. It is essential for successful tactical planning.
   C. It minimizes the need for communication.
   D. It ensures rapid movement of troops.

12. Which ground is described as "easy to travel but dangerous in the locality of the enemy"?

   A. Broken Ground
   B. Flat and Open Ground
   C. High Ground
   D. Dead Ground

13. Which type of ground affords protection from flat path weapons but not from air or high path weapons?

   A. Flat and Open Ground
   B. High Ground
   C. Dead Ground
   D. Broken Ground

14. What should a section commander continuously do while on the move?

    A. Focus on speed
    B. Explain the ground to his men
    C. Maintain silence
    D. Conserve ammunition

15. One of the following is NOT used while describing ground?

    A. Using landmarks
    B. Dividing the ground by distance
    C. Drawing a detailed map
    D. Giving left and right boundaries

16. The main purpose of dividing ground into foreground, middle distance, and distance is__________.

    A. To enhance the speed of movement
    B. To simplify the description and understanding of the area
    C. To reduce the number of landmarks needed
    D. To facilitate the use of heavy artillery

1. D	2. B	3. B	4. D	5. B	6. B	7. B	8. C	9. B	10. C
11. B	12. B	13. D	14. B	15. C	16. B				

3.3 RECOGNITION, DESCRIPTION, INDICATION OF LAND MARK AND TARGET

1. What is the main objective of 'Recognition and Description of Targets' in Field Craft?

    A. To improve physical stamina
    B. To enhance communication skills

C. To accurately identify and describe enemy positions
D. To practice advanced combat maneuvers

2. What is a landmark?

A. A natural feature used for navigation
B. An important object on the ground used in verbal orders to explain the ground
C. A military structure used for defense
D. An object with technical significance indicated to bring down fire

3. Which method is NOT used for indicating targets?

A. Indication by Description
B. Indication by Range
C. Indication by Color
D. Indication by Direction

4. What is a reference point?

A. A point on a map used for navigation.
B. An important and unmistakable object used to indicate other landmarks or targets.
C. A position marked for artillery fire.
D. A specific coordinate in GPS.

5. In the indication by range method, how is a target typically described?

A. By mentioning its color and size.
B. By providing a numerical distance to the target.
C. By indicating the direction first and then the range.
D. By using a reference point and its coordinates.

6. What is an 'easy targets'?

    A. Targets that can be indicated without any aids.
    B. Targets that require a detailed description for recognition.
    C. Targets that are always visible and noticeable.
    D. Targets indicated by using direction and range together.

7. Which degree corresponds to 'Three Quarter Left/Right' in the direction method?

    A. Approximately 10 degrees
    B. Approximately 45 degrees
    C. Approximately 22 ½ degrees
    D. Approximately 67 ½ degrees

8. Why is the accurate indication of targets being important in battle?

    A. It helps in creating maps.
    B. It ensures that targets are understood and recognized by the troops.
    C. It is used for training purposes only.
    D. It is necessary for setting up defense mechanisms.

9. How does the direction method used to indicate difficult targets?

    A. Color codes
    B. Symbols
    C. The general line of direction, a known reference point, or another landmark
    D. GPS coordinates

10. While indicating target, what does 'Full Left/Right' represent?

    A. Approximately 45 degrees
    B. Approximately 67 ½ degrees
    C. Approximately 90 degrees
    D. Approximately 22 ½ degrees

11. Match the following directions with their corresponding measuring degrees

Direction	Measuring Degrees
A. Slight Left/Right	1. Approximately 22 ½ degrees
B. Quarter Left/Right	2. Approximately 67 ½ degrees
C. Half Left/Right	3. Approximately 10 degrees
D. Three Quarter Left/Right	4. Approximately 90 degrees
E. Full Left/Right	5. Approximately 45 degrees

A. A3, B1, C5, D2, E4
B. A1, B3, C2, D4, E5
C. A2, B4, C1, D3, E5
D. A5, B1, C4, D3, E2

1. C	2. B	3. C	4. B	5. B	6. A	7. D	8. B	9. C	10. C
11. A									

3.4 OBSERVATION, CAMOUFLAGE AND CONCEALMENT

1. Which factor is NOT considered when determining why objects are visible in daylight?

   A. Shape
   B. Shine
   C. Sound
   D. Shadow

2. What does 'Fire and Move' involve in the Field Craft?

   A. Establishing defensive positions
   B. Simultaneously advancing and providing covering fire
   C. Using stealth to approach the enemy
   D. Setting up ambush points

3. What does personal camouflage involve?

   A. The use of artillery to disguise movements
   B. The use of terrain features to hide equipment
   C. The use of disruptive patterns, clothing, and local vegetation
   D. The coordination of troop movements under cover of darkness

4. The term "camouflage" originates from which language?

   A. Latin
   B. German
   C. French
   D. Spanish

5. Which of the following is not a factor that makes objects visible?

   A. Shape
   B. Shine
   C. Movement
   D. Weight

6. Which type of cover protects from both view and fire?

   A. Cover from view
   B. Camouflage net
   C. Cover from fire
   D. Personal concealment

7. Which of the following is not a part of personal camouflage?

   A. Camouflaging the face
   B. Using disruptive pattern clothing
   C. Wearing bright, reflective gear
   D. Using local vegetation

8. Which factor does NOT make objects visible during the day?

   A. Shape
   B. Sound
   C. Shine
   D. Shadow

9. How should a soldier's equipment be camouflaged?

   A. By painting it bright colors
   B. By covering it with natural materials and breaking its outline
   C. By leaving it exposed
   D. By using it as a decoy

1. C	2. B	3. C	4. C	5. D	6. C	7. C	8. B	9. B

3.4 FIELD SIGNALS

1. Hand signal for 'Advance' is__________.

   A. Right arm fully extended above head and waved from side to side
   B. Right arm swung from rear to front in an under-arm motion
   C. Right arm raised to full extent above head
   D. Right hand placed on top of the head

2. To get the attention of troops which field signal is used?

   A. Blowing a whistle
   B. Using a flashlight
   C. Shouting commands
   D. Throwing a rock

3. Field signal of "a succession of short blasts on a whistle" signify/ used for indicating__________.

   A. Enemy aircraft departed
   B. Cautionary signal
   C. Enemy aircraft approaching
   D. Alarm blast

4. Which filed signal indicates 'Enemy Approaching'?

   A. Both hands open, palm inwards at waist level with inwards scooping motion
   B. Right arm raised and bent above head
   C. Punching motion with right or left hand
   D. Both hands crossed in front of the body at waist level

5. Field signals primarily used for __________ purpose in battle?

   A. To distract the enemy
   B. To give orders and control troops when voice control is not possible
   C. To mark territory
   D. To identify friendly forces

6. Which of the following is NOT a correct method of field signal used to get the attention of troops?

   A. A short blast of whistle
   B. Shouting loudly

C. A bird call
D. Clicks by fingers

7. Which of the following method is used for field signals at night?

A. Use of flags
B. Flashing torch in Morse code
C. Mercury coated mirrors
D. Pre-decided signals on a walkie-talkie

8. Which field signal method is NOT used to attract the attention of troops?

A. A short blast of whistle.
B. A bird call
C. Flashing a torch
D. Clicks by fingers

9. Which operations require utmost silence?

A. Battle noises
B. Dispatch Runners
C. Ambush, patrolling, raid, cordon
D. Use of rope and blacked out torch

10. Which of the following field signal is used for visual signals during the day?

A. Use of rope
B. Use of blacked out torch
C. Flags and mercury coated mirrors
D. Firing of weapon

11. During day for the purpose of field signal which coloured flags are used?

    A. Red, Green, and Yellow
    B. Red, Green, and White
    C. Blue, Green, and White
    D. Red, Yellow, and Black

12. Which Filed signal is used at night?

    A. Mercury coated mirrors
    B. Clothes superficially hung out to dry
    C. Use of blacked out torch
    D. Flashing of torch in Morse Code

13. Why might voice control not be possible during a battle?

    A. Due to the high noise from firing and vehicle movement.
    B. The need for utmost silence during certain operations.
    C. Intervening distances are too large.
    D. All of the above.

14. Which of the following is NOT a means of communication in the army?

    A. Dispatch runners.
    B. Mercury coated mirrors.
    C. Radio sets.
    D. Dispatch rider.

15. Match the following

Name of Signal	Signals with Hand
A. Cautionary Blast	1. A short blast to draw attention to a signal or order about to be given.
B. The Alarm Blast	2. A succession of alternate long and short whistle blasts.
C. Enemy Aircraft	3. A succession of short blasts.
D. Enemy Aircraft departed	4. Two long blasts repeated at interval of five seconds.

A. A4, B3, C2, D1
B. A2, B3, C4, D1
C. A1, B2, C3, D4
D. A3, B2, C1, D4

1. B	2. A	3. C	4. A	5. B	6. B	7. D	8. C	9. C	10. C
11. B	12. C	13. D	14. B	15. C					

3.5 SECTION FORMATION

1. What is the smallest subunit of an Infantry Battalion is?

A. Platoon
B. Company
C. Section
D. Brigade

2. How many members are there in a section of an Infantry Battalion?

A. 8
B. 10
C. 12
D. 15

3. A section is organized in to _________ and _________ groups.

   A. Platoon group and Support group
   B. Rifle group and Support group
   C. Command group and Signal group
   D. Assault group and Defense group

4. What is the primary difference between the Rifle group and the Support group within a section?

   A. The Rifle group carries heavier weapons
   B. The Support group provides direct fire support to the Rifle group
   C. The Rifle group is responsible for communication
   D. The Support group handles all reconnaissance duties

5. Which section formation is typically used when maximum fire is required quickly?

   A. Single file formation
   B. Arrow head formation
   C. Extended line formation
   D. Diamond formation

6. What are the basic factors that determine the type of section formation to be adopted?

   A. Number of troops and terrain type
   B. Degree of control required, type of ground, necessity of bringing down maximum fire, and task
   C. Type of weapons available and enemy strength
   D. Time of day and weather conditions

7. What is the role of scouts in section formations?

A. To provide medical aid
B. To carry extra ammunition
C. To act as the eyes and ears of the section
D. To handle communications

8. Which formation is characterized by a straight line of soldiers?

A. File Formation
B. Diamond Formation
C. Arrow Head Formation
D. Extended Line Formation

9. Who are considered the eyes and ears of the section?

A. Commanders
B. Scouts
C. Support group
D. Rifle group

10. In which formation do soldiers form a V-shape?

A. File Formation
B. Diamond Formation
C. Arrow Head Formation
D. Extended Line Formation

1. C	2. B	3. B	4. B	5. C	6. B	7. C	8. A	9. B	10. C

3.6 FIRE CONTROL ORDER

1. GRIT stands for__________.

A. Group, Range, Indication of target and Type of fire
B. Growth, Resilience, Integrity, and Tenacity
C. Group, Rapid action indication of target fire
D. Group Rolled into Trench

2. Which of the following is a correct sequence of fire control order?

   A. GRIT B. GTIR C. GIRT D. GRTI

3. Match the following terminologies used in fire control order

Terms	Directions
A. Fire Unit	1. Which is the area over which it can fire effectively.
B. Fire Direction Orders	2. Area of ground for which the fire unit is responsible and engage targets
C. Fire Control Orders	3. Usually a Section
D. Arc of Fire	4. Orders given by the fire unit commander
E. Field of fire	5. Orders which the fire unit commander receives from his superior

   A. A3, B5, C4, D2, E1 C. A3, B4, C5, D2, E1
   B. A3, B5, C4, D1, E2 D. A3, B5, C1, D2, E1

4. Match the following Types of Fire Control Orders

Fire Control Orders	Direction of use
A. Delayed Fire	1. When the target is not continuously seen by everyone in the section or when the enemy has taken cover

B. Full Fire	2. When the time is not available to give out a full fire order
C. Opportunity Fire	3. When fire is to be brought down immediately on a target within the effective range of weapons.
D. Brief Fire	4. When enemy is seen approaching at a longer range so that necessary preparations are made by the troops to open fire

A. A3, B1, C4, D2
B. A4, B2, C3, D1
C. A3, B4, C1, D2
D. A4, B3, C1, D2

5. Which fire control order has to be given when "Time is not available" to issue a full fire order?

   A. Delayed fire control orders
   B. Full fire control orders
   C. Opportunity fire control orders
   D. Brief fire control orders

6. What is the main purpose of fire control orders?

   A. To ensure maximum noise during battle
   B. To control the fire of a section for effective engagement
   C. To signal retreat
   D. To practice firing discipline

7. Which of the following is essential for effective fire discipline and control in Field Craft?

   A. Opening fire at the earliest possible moment
   B. Using the heaviest weapon available
   C. Ensuring the enemy is engaged effectively with controlled fire
   D. Using as much ammunition as possible to intimidate the enemy

8. When is fire and movement tactics mainly used?

   A. During training exercises
   B. When the enemy has opened effective small arms fire
   C. For ceremonial parades
   D. For logistics and supply chain management

9. What is the function of fire control orders?

   A. To direct artillery fire
   B. To control the fire of a section by ensuring effective engagement and judicious use of ammunition
   C. To communicate with air support
   D. To organize logistical support

10. What should a commander avoid to prevent disclosing their position prematurely?

   A. Moving silently
   B. Giving clear signals
   C. Opening fire too early or at too great a range
   D. Using camouflage

11. What is the purpose of Fire Discipline and Control?

    A. Ensuring all soldiers can fire at will
    B. Managing and directing fire to avoid waste and increase effectiveness
    C. Training in physical fitness
    D. Practicing marksmanship regularly

1. A	2. A	3. A	4. D	5. D	6. B	7. C	8. B	9. B	10. C	11. B

3.7 FIRE AND MOVEMENT

1. What is the primary aim of infantry?

    A. To defend strategic points
    B. To close in with the enemy and destroy him
    C. To provide reconnaissance
    D. To secure supplies

2. In which of the following scenarios should fire and movement tactics be used?

    A. When the enemy is retreating
    B. When the enemy has opened effective small arms (SA) fire
    C. When crossing an open field at night
    D. When setting up a defensive position

3. What is the main purpose of "Fire and Movement" tactics?

    A. To retreat safely from the enemy
    B. To allow troops to move while keeping the enemy suppressed
    C. To build defensive structures
    D. To communicate with other units

4. When should covering fire be used?

   A. Only when it is dark
   B. When moving in open ground
   C. When enemy forces are retreating
   D. During peaceful negotiations

5. Which type of cover provides both protection from view and from fire?

   A. Hedges and bushes
   B. Open fields
   C. Sunken roads and ditches
   D. Isolated trees

6. Which is NOT a common mistake during fire and movement?

   A. Unfolding a map in the open
   B. Using a covered approach to an Observation Post
   C. Using conspicuous landmarks
   D. Halting near mapped features

7. What should be the priority when selecting a fire position?

   A. Proximity to enemy lines
   B. Providing cover from fire and view
   C. Ease of communication
   D. Availability of supplies

8. What is "dead ground" in military terms?

   A. Ground where no enemy fire can reach
   B. Ground that cannot be seen from a particular position
   C. Ground that is highly visible to the enemy
   D. Ground that is completely flat

9. Which type of ground is safest from enemy observed fire but not from indirect fire?

   A. Open fields
   B. Dead ground
   C. Elevated positions
   D. Forest clearings

10. Troops should avoid doing _________ when they are near enemy lines.

   A. Using maps and compasses
   B. Moving during daylight
   C. Halting near road or track junctions
   D. Using natural cover

11. What is an important factor in the fire control during an attack?

   A. Immediate fire effect
   B. Establishing defensive positions
   C. Conserving ammunition
   D. Reducing noise

12. Which cover type can give protection from enemy air and ground observation?

   A. Hedges and bushes
   B. Woods
   C. Open fields
   D. Streams and ditches

13. What is the limitation of using air photographs for reconnaissance?

   A. They are more up-to-date than maps
   B. They show the size and shape of features accurately
   C. They provide complete geographical cover
   D. They are expensive to produce

1. B	2. B	3. B	4. B	5. C	6. B	7. B	8. B	9. B	10. C
11. A	12. B	13. D							

3.8 KNOTS AND LASHINGS

1. What is the purpose of a "Thumb Knot"?

   A. To create a loop that will not slip
   B. To prevent the rope end from fraying
   C. To securely join two ropes of equal thickness
   D. To secure a rope to a spar

2. Which knot is used to join two springy materials together?

   A. Reef Knot
   B. Thief Knot
   C. Fisherman's Knot
   D. Clove Hitch

3. Which of the following is a "Bowline Knot"?

   A. Making a stop on a rope end
   B. Forming a loop that will not slip
   C. Securing a rope to a spar
   D. Joining two ropes of equal thickness

4. What is the use of a "Clove Hitch Knot"?

   A. To form a loop that will not slip
   B. To join two ropes of equal thickness
   C. To secure a rope to a spar
   D. To prevent a rope end from fraying

5. Which knot can be easily undone and is more ornamental than a thumb knot?

   A. Overhand Knot
   B. Figure Eight
   C. Reef Knot
   D. Fisherman's Knot

6. Which knot was often used by sailors to tie their sea chests?

   A. Reef Knot
   B. Thief Knot
   C. Fisherman's Knot
   D. Bowline

7. What is the primary use of lashings?

   A. To create loops in ropes
   B. To secure a rope end
   C. To join two ropes of different thickness
   D. To join poles together

8. What is the main benefit of learning various types of knots and lashings?

   A. They are ornamental and decorative
   B. They help in climbing and rappelling activities
   C. They can be used to create fishing nets
   D. They are mainly for competitive purposes

9. Which letter is used to denote the free or untied end of the rope?

   A. R B. F C. S D. T

10. Which knot is suitable for wire fishing gut or vines?

    A. Reef Knot
    B. Thief Knot
    C. Fisherman's Knot
    D. Bowline

11. Which letter is used to denote the Standing or secured end?

    A. R B. F C. S D. T

1. B	2. C	3. B	4. C	5. B	6. B	7. B	8. B	9. B	10. C
11. C									

04
Communication

4.1 TYPES OF COMMUNICATION

1. Who invented the "Telephone"?

   A. Thomas Alva Edison
   B. Alexander Graham Bell
   C. Alexander Fleming
   D. Amos Dolbear

2. Which of the following scientist invented "Radio"?

   A. Guglielmo Marconi
   B. Heinrich Hertz
   C. Niels Bohr
   D. Christian Huygenes

3. Radio Telephony is used for

   A. Simple one-way voice communication
   B. Two-way voice communication
   C. For testing voice
   D. Multi communication at a time

4. Radio telegraphy is used for

   A. Transmission of message and key conversations
   B. Transmission of signals
   C. Transmission of voice
   D. Transmission of mechanical wave

5. Which type of communication is described as "the basic means of signal communication for a force which is static"?

   A. Radio Communication
   B. Line Communication
   C. Net Radio
   D. Radio Relay

6. One of the main advantages of line communication is is__________.

   A. It is highly flexible once laid
   B. It is relatively secure
   C. It is quick to construct
   D. It is highly mobile

7. Which type of radio wave propagation is used for long-distance communication, often up to 300 km?

   A. Sky Wave Propagation
   B. Ground Wave Propagation
   C. Space Wave Propagation
   D. Tropospheric Scatter

8. What is tropospheric scatter?

   A. Method of communicating with microwave radio signals
   B. Method of communicating with Nano wave radio signals
   C. Method of scattering of light in troposphere
   D. Method of scattered communication in earths atmosphere

9. Which type of communication involves using a series of radio transmitters and receivers normally spaced 20-35 kms apart?

   A. Line Communication
   B. Radio Relay
   C. Net Radio
   D. Ground Wave Propagation

10. Which is NOT an advantage of net radio?

    A. Vulnerable only at terminal points
    B. Flexible and can be rapidly rearranged
    C. Highly secure from enemy interception
    D. Economical in personnel and equipment

11. Which type of wave travels through a vacuum of outer space?

    A. Mechanical Waves
    B. Electromagnetic Waves
    C. Ground Waves
    D. Space Waves

12. What is the major disadvantage of line communication?

    A. It is relatively secure
    B. It is flexible once constructed
    C. It is vulnerable to physical interference
    D. It is economical

13. What does radio communication require to transmit and receive messages?

    A. Only a radio transmitter
    B. Only a radio receiver
    C. Both transmitting and receiving equipment
    D. A local loop and trunk

14. Which is the basic means of signal communication for any mobile force?

    A. Line Communication
    B. Net Radio
    C. Radio Relay
    D. Sky Wave Propagation

15. Which factor does NOT significantly affect the efficiency of net radio communication?

    A. Weather
    B. Power output of the set
    C. Terrain
    D. Type of transmitting antenna

16. What does the local loop in line communication refer to?

    A. A type of radio wave
    B. A method of securing communication
    C. The connection from the user to the end office
    D. A type of electromagnetic wave

17. What is one advantage of radio relay over line communication?

    A. It is less expensive
    B. It is quicker to set up and move
    C. It does not require any equipment
    D. It is completely secure

18. What type of communication uses radio waves that travel in a straight line?

    A. Ground Wave Propagation
    B. Space Wave Propagation
    C. Sky Wave Propagation
    D. Tropospheric Scatter

19. Which type of wave propagation is limited by the curvature of the Earth?

    A. Sky Wave Propagation
    B. Space Wave Propagation
    C. Ground Wave Propagation
    D. Mechanical Wave Propagation

20. What is the disadvantage of radio communication?

    A. It is highly flexible
    B. It requires no maintenance
    C. It is susceptible to enemy interception
    D. It provides secure communication

1. A	2. A	3. A	4.	5. B	6. B	7. D	8. A	9. B	10. C
11. B	12. C	13. C	14. B	15. D	16. C	17.B	18. B	19. B	20. C

4.2 CHARACTERISTICS OF WIRELESS TECHNOLOGY (MOBILE, WI-FI ETC)

1. Which of the following is a key benefit of Wi-Fi technology?

   A. Requires professional installation for setup
   B. Provides unmatched mobility and flexibility
   C. Needs a wired connection for internet access
   D. Limited to short-range communication only

2. When did the development on Wi-Fi technology begin?

   A. 1985 B. 1997 C. 2000 D. 2010

3. Which organization introduced the 802.11 technologies?

   A. ISO B. IEEE C. ITU D. FCC

4. How Wi-Fi transmits data between its nodes?

   A. Fiber optic cables
   B. Satellite signals
   C. Bluetooth
   D. Radio network

5. What is a major benefit of Wi-Fi?

   A. Requires wires for connection
   B. Limited to home use only
   C. Allows mobility without wires
   D. Slower than conventional modems

6. Wi-Fi networks are made up of _________ to provide coverage.

   A. Antennas
   B. Satellites
   C. Cells
   D. Towers

7. Which feature of Wi-Fi permits long-range communication?

   A. Wired operations
   B. Wireless operations
   C. Bluetooth
   D. Cellular network

8. What type of devices can Wi-Fi technology connect?

   A. Only computers
   B. Only phones
   C. Various devices like games, MP3 players, and PDAs
   D. Only TVs

9. Where can you typically find Wi-Fi hotspots?

   A. Only in homes
   B. Only in offices
   C. In public places, homes, and offices
   D. Only in schools

10. How does Wi-Fi compare to DSL and cable connections in terms of speed?

    A. Slower
    B. Same speed
    C. Faster
    D. Depends on the provider

11. The call quality of Wi-Fi technology greatly influenced by ________.

    A. Data plan
    B. Type of phone used
    C. Electromagnetic radiation from household appliances
    D. Time of day

12. Why Wi-Fi is considered as convenient?

    A. Only works with cables
    B. Automatically connects to the internet near a hotspot
    C. Requires specific locations for setup
    D. Limited to a single device

13. What is the limitation of Wi-Fi technology?

    A. Requires a lot of power
    B. Cannot be used with mobile devices
    C. Compatibility issues between different manufacturers' devices
    D. Only supports short-range communication

14. Which advantage does Wi-Fi offer?

    A. Requires expensive installation
    B. Involves high maintenance costs
    C. Reduces cost due to absence of wires and cables
    D. Requires monthly subscription fees

15. The security issue concerned with Wi-Fi is__________.

    A. Difficult to set up
    B. Requires a lot of power
    C. Wireless transmissions can pass through walls
    D. Cannot connect multiple devices

16. True statement for 'wireless reception' for Wi-Fi is __________.

    A. Consistent everywhere
    B. Varies from area to area
    C. Always strong in apartments
    D. Only works outdoors

1. B	2. B	3. B	4. D	5. C	6. C	7. B	8. C	9. C	10. C
11. C	12. B	13. C	14. C	15. C	16. B				

4.3 CHARACTERISTICS OF WALKIE/TALKIE

1. Who invented walkie-talkie during the Second World War?

    A. Alexander Graham Bell
    B. Donald L. Hings, Alfred J. Gross
    C. Thomas Edison
    D. Nikola Tesla

2. What is the main difference between a walkie-talkie's speaker and a phone's earpiece?

   A. A walkie-talkie's speaker can be heard only by the user.
   B. A phone's earpiece can be heard by those in the user's immediate vicinity.
   C. A walkie-talkie's speaker can be heard by the user and those in the user's immediate vicinity.
   D. There is no difference.

3. Match the following features of GP338 Motorola radio set

1. Frequency range VHF mode	A. 128 channels
2. Communication range	B. 403 MHz to 470 MHz
3. Frequency range UHF mode	C. 4 to 5 Km
4. Channels	D. 136 MHz to 174 MHz

   A. 1B, 2C, 3D, 4A C. 1C, 2B, 3D,4A
   B. 1D, 2C, 3B, 4A D. D, 2B, 3C, 4A

4. What is the main purpose of the selective call facility in the GP338 Motorola radio set?

   A. To adjust the volume
   B. To change the battery
   C. To make private calls to specific units
   D. To switch between UHF and VHF modes

5. What is the function of the scan operation on the GP338 Motorola radio set?

   A. To lock the keypad
   B. To search and monitor channels
   C. To adjust the brightness of the LCD display
   D. To increase battery life

6. How many characters can the LCD display window of the GP338 Motorola radio set show?

   A. 10 characters
   B. 12 characters
   C. 14 characters
   D. 16 characters

1. B	2. C	3. B	4. C	5. B	6. C

4.4 BASIC RADIO TELEPHONY (RT) PROCEDURE

1. What is the primary purpose of Radio Telephony (RT) procedure?

   A. To make radio conversations entertaining
   B. To ensure secure and successful communication
   C. To reduce the cost of radio equipment

2. What is a key advantage of RT procedure?

   A. It is easier to intercept
   B. It is flexible and easy to establish
   C. It requires skilled operators
   D. It is liable to atmospheric interference

3. In the principles of Radio Telephony Procedure, the 'B' in BASS stands for__________.

   A. Brevity
   B. Basic
   C. Broadcast
   D. Bandwidth

4. Which type of RT communication involves a conversation that is not registered?

   A. RT Conversation
   B. Unregistered (UR) Message
   C. Formal Message
   D. Code Sign

5. What is the role of a Control Station in a Radio Net?

   A. To interfere with other stations
   B. To serve as the senior HQ and maintain radio discipline
   C. To change frequencies frequently
   D. To transmit weather reports

6. What does the term 'Link Sign' refer to in RT procedure?

   A. A nickname used for convenience
   B. A group of letters or figures to conceal the identity of a station
   C. A standard phrase used in RT communication
   D. The main frequency used for communication

7. Which standard RT phrase means "Message received and understood"?

   A. Wilco B. Roger C. Over D. Out

8. What does the standard RT phrase 'Wilco' mean?

   A. Message received, understood, and will be complied with
   B. Message received and acknowledged
   C. Transmission has ended and I expect to hear from you
   D. Pause for a few seconds

9. What type of call addresses all stations on a net except a few specified ones?

   A. Single Call
   B. Net Call
   C. Multiple Calls
   D. Net Call with Exceptions

10. What should be done when there is bad weather during radio communication?

    A. Change the link signs
    B. Use jargon to ensure clarity
    C. Establish communication again
    D. Switch off the radio

1. B	2. B	3. A	4. A	5. B	6. B	7. B	8. A	9. D	10. C

4.5 LATEST TRENDS AND DEVELOPMENT IN COMMUNICATION

1. What frequency bands are used in troposcatter communication systems?

   A. Low Frequency (LF) and Medium Frequency (MF)
   B. Medium Frequency (MF) and High Frequency (HF)
   C. Very High Frequency (VHF) and Ultra High Frequency (UHF)
   D. Ultra High Frequency (UHF) and Super High Frequency (SHF)

2. What is the typical range covered by troposcatter communication systems?

   A. 1 Km to 10 Km
   B. 70 Km to 1000 Km
   C. 10 Km to 50 Km
   D. 1000 Km to 5000 Km

3. The tropospheric region of the atmosphere is located below which height?

   A. 5 Km B. 10 Km C. 15 Km D. 20 Km

4. What is the function of a modem (Modulator-Demodulator)?

   A. To amplify signals for long-distance communication
   B. To convert digital signals into analog signals and vice versa for transmission over telephone lines
   C. To encrypt and decrypt data for secure communication
   D. To connect multiple devices within a local area network

5. Which of the following statements about FAX (FACSIMILE) is NOT true?

   A. It can transmit both graphics and alphanumeric information
   B. It eliminates the need for any transmission medium
   C. It reduces time and eliminates transmission errors
   D. It can use various transmission media such as telephone lines and microwave radio waves

6. What is TELEX (Tele Printer Exchange)?

   A. Communication devices which exchange information between two such instruments
   B. Communication devices which exchange information between different devices

C. Printer, which exchange printed information only
D. Monitor which display the message in case a call is disconnected

7. Which of the following country helped India to launch its first satellite, Aryabhatta?

A. USA
B. China
C. United Kingdom
D. Soviet Union

8. What is a satellite?

A. An object which revolves around another larger object and generates its own power
B. An object which revolves around another larger object whose motion is primarily and permanently determined by the force of attraction of the body
C. An object which carries astronauts to the space for space research and exploration
D. Spherical bodies lands on other planets while revolving

9. Which of the following is the India's first satellite and when it was launched?

A. Bhaskara, 7June, 1979
B. Aryabhatta, 19 April, 1975
C. Rohini, 25 APril, 1975
D. INSAT, 10 April, 1978

10. World's first man made satellite launched in space was__________.

A. Apollo
B. Sputnik
C. Bhaskara
D. Dong Fang Hong

11. What is a key feature of multimedia technology?

    A. It only displays text information
    B. It only uses sound and graphics without video
    C. It combines video, sound, graphics, and text with user interaction
    D. It is only used for video conferencing

12. One the key advantage of optical fiber communication is__________.

    A. High power requirement
    B. Large cable size
    C. No electromagnetic interference
    D. Cheap equipment and manufacturing

13. The term "Internet" refers to__________.

    A. A single large computer
    B. A local network within a building
    C. A collection of individual data networks connected globally
    D. A type of multimedia technology

14. Which of the following is NOT an advantage of a computer system?

    A. Speed of process and calculations
    B. Mass storage of data
    C. Data loss if machine malfunctions
    D. Accuracy of process and calculation once the program is proved

1. D	2. B	3. C	4. B	5. B	6. A	7. D	8. B	9. B	10. B
11. C	12. C	13. C	14. C						

05

Military History

1. Why the ideology of understanding an enemy is important?

   A. It helps in developing manpower
   B. It provides tools to prepare for current and future wars
   C. It enhances metal strength
   D. It fosters economic development.

2. What is the primary focus of military history?

   A. To know Cultural practices
   B. To know armed conflicts and their impacts
   C. To know about Economic invasions
   D. Enhance medical advancements

3. Why the study of military history is important?

   A. It promotes joining into military
   B. It provides lessons from past conflicts.
   C. It focuses on economics
   D. It is purely for entertainment

4. Which regiment did K.M Cariappa join as a Temporary Second Lieutenant?

   A. 37 (Prince of Wales) Dogra
   B. 2nd Queen Victoria's Own Rajput Light Infantry
   C. Carnatic Infantry
   D. 1st Gorkha Rifles

5. K.M Cariappa lead the Indian forces on the Western Front in ________ In conflict/

   A. Indo-Pakistan War of 1947-48
   B. Indo-Pakistan War of 1965
   C. Indo-China War of 1962
   D. Indo-Pakistan War of 1971

6. Which regiment did Sam Manekshaw join after posted to the British battalion?

   A. 16th Punjab Regiment
   B. 2nd Queen Victoria's Own Rajput Light Infantry
   C. 8th Gorkha Rifles
   D. 54th Sikhs

7. What was Sam Manekshaw's popular nickname?

   A. Kipper
   B. Sher-e-Punjab
   C. Sam the Brave
   D. Sher-e-Mysore

8. K.M Cariappa received ________ award for his services in Burma.

   A. Padma Bhushan
   B. Military Cross
   C. Officer of the Order of the British Empire
   D. Legion of Merit

9. What was the result of 1971 Indo-Pakistan War?

   A. Independence of Baluchistan
   B. Liberation of Bangladesh
   C. Creation of Pakistan
   D. Signing of the Treaty of Versailles

10. On which date the "Instrument of Surrender" signed to end the 1971 Indo-Pakistan War?

A. 16 December 1971
B. 26 January 1971
C. 15 August 1971
D. 3 June 1971

11. Who pinned the Military Cross ribbon to Sam Manekshaw after he was severely wounded?

A. Major General David Cowan
B. General Douglas MacArthur
C. Field Marshal Bernard Montgomery
D. General Dwight D. Eisenhower

12. Which key position captured in Burma during World War II by Sam Manekshaw's company?

A. Pagoda Hill
B. Red Hill
C. Blue Mountain
D. Tiger Hill

13. What significant role did Sam Manekshaw played in the 1971 Indo-Pakistani War?

A. Ari Chief Marshal
B. Admiral
C. Chief of the Army Staff
D. Chief Commander

1. B	2. B	3. C	4. C	5. A	6. D	7. C	8. C	9. B	10. A
11. A	12. A	13. C							

5.1 INDIAN ARMY WAR HEROES PVC

1. Identify the correct statements for the Param Vir Chakra (PVC)?

   I. Highest non-gallantry award in India
   II. Similar to USA's Medal of honour and UK's Victoria cross
   III. Highest military decoration for valour or self-sacrifice
   IV. All government servants are eligible for the award

   A. I and IV
   B. I and III
   C. II and III
   D. All are correct

2. Which of the following are correct for the Param Vir Chakra (PVC) award?

   I. Peace time
   II. War time
   III. In the face of enemy
   IV. Off the face of enemy.

   A. I and IV
   B. II and III
   C. I, II, III and IV
   D. I, II and III

3. When was the Param Vir Chakra (PVC) established?

   A. 15 August 1947
   B. 26 January 1950
   C. 2 October 1950
   D. 26 January 1947

4. Who designed the Param Vir Chakra medal?

   A. Savitri Khanolkar
   B. Lata Mangeshkar
   C. Radhika Apte
   D. Rani Laxmi Bai

5. How many times the Param Vir Chakra hasbeen awarded?

   A. 10 times
   B. 15 times
   C. 21 times
   D. 30 times

6. How many of the PVC awards were posthumous?

   A. 5 B. 10 C. 14 D. 20

7. Who captured a Pakistani medium machine-gun post during the Indo-Pakistani War 1947?

   A. Vikram Batra
   B. Shaitan Singh
   C. Piru Singh
   D. Abdul Hamid

8. Where was Company Havildar Major Piru Singh born?

   A. Jodhpur, Rajasthan
   B. Beri, Rajasthan
   C. Palampur, Himachal Pradesh
   D. Delhi

9. During which battle Major Shaitan Singh showed exemplary courage and leadership?

   A. Battle of Rezang La
   B. Battle of Longewala
   C. Battle of Point 4875
   D. Battle of Hilli

10. In which sector Rezang La located?

    A. Kashmir
    B. Siachen
    C. Arunachal Pradesh
    D. Chushul

11. How the fellow soldiers used to call Captain Vikram Batra during the Kargil War __________?

    A. Tiger
    B. Lion
    C. Sher Shah
    D. Eagle

12. When did Major Shaitan Singh died?

    A. 7 July 1999
    B. 18 July 1948
    C. 18 November 1962
    D. 20 June 1999

13. Which award was given to Major Shaitan Singh, posthumously for his bravery?

A. Maha Vir Chakra
B. Ashoka Chakra
C. Param Vir Chakra
D. Vir Chakra

14. Which regiment did Captain Vikram Batra belong to?

A. 6th Rajputana Rifles
B. 13 Jammu & Kashmir Rifles
C. 1st Punjab Regiment
D. 13 Kumaon

15. What were the last words of Captain Vikram Batra?

A. "Jai Hind"
B. "Jai Mata Di"
C. "Vande Mataram"
D. "Bharat Mata Ki Jai"

16. What is the English translation of Piru Singh's battle cry "Raja Ramchandra Ki Jai"?

A. Long Live India
B. Hail Lord Rama
C. Victory to the Brave
D. Hail the King

17. Company Havildar Major Piru Singh was a part of __________ unit during the Indo-Pakistani War 1947.

A. 1st Punjab Regiment
B. 13 Jammu & Kashmir Rifles
C. 13 Kumaon
D. 6th Rajputana Rifles

18. Who was the first Adjutant General responsible for the establishment of the PVC?

A. Major General Hira Lal
B. Major General Arjun Singh

C. Major General Ranjit Singh
D. Major General Vikram Khanolkar

19. Major Shaitan Singh born in which year?

A. 1924 B. 1925 C. 1936 D. 1939

20. In which operation Captain Vikram Batra recaptured peak 5140?

A. Operation Meghdoot
B. Operation Pawan
C. Operation Vijay
D. Operation Rakshak

1. C	2. B	3. B	4. A	5. C	6. C	7. C	8. B	9. A	10. D
11. C	12. C	13. C	14. B	15. B	16. B	17. D	18. A	19. A	20. C

5.2 STUDY OF BATTLES OF INDO-PAK WAR 1965, 1971 & KARGIL

1. Which event led to the partition of the subcontinent in 1947?

A. The end of World War II
B. The Cold War
C. Indian independence
D. The formation of the United Nations

2. When did India got independence?

A. 14 August 1947
B. 15 August 1947
C. January 1950
D. 2 October 1948

3. The primary cause of 1965 Indo-Pak war_________.

A. Disputes over Punjab
B. Disputes over Kashmir
C. Disputes over Bengal
D. Disputes over Sindh

4. Operation launched by Pakistan in August 1965 was __________.

   A. Operation Vijay
   B. Operation Grand Slam
   C. Operation Gibraltar
   D. Operation Blue Star

5. Which battle is known as the largest tank battle since World War II?

   A. Battle of Longewala1965
   B. Battle of Asal Uttar1965
   C. Battle of Chawinda1965
   D. Battle of Dograi1965

6. What was the result of the Battle of Dograi in 1965?

   A. Capture of Lahore
   B. Capture of Dograi
   C. Ceasefire announcement
   D. Indian withdrawal

7. Reason for triggering Indo-Pakistan War 1971 was __________.

   A. Refugee crisis from East Pakistan
   B. Refugee crisis from West Pakistan
   C. Disputes over Kashmir
   D. Disputes over Punjab

8. In the 1971 Indo-Pakistan war, India took stand to support __________ group

   A. Northern Alliance
   B. Mukti Bahini
   C. Taliban
   D. Naxalites

9. Name of the key air operation launched by Pakistan in December 1971?

   A. Operation Vijay
   B. Operation Grand Slam
   C. Operation Chengiz Khan
   D. Operation Gibraltar

10. The Battle of Longewala held at_________.

    A. Punjab B. Rajasthan C. Kashmir C. Bengal

11. How many Pakistani tanks were destroyed in the Battle of Longewala?

    A. 10 B. 20 C. 38 D. 50

12. When did the Pakistani Army surrender in Dhaka during the 1971 war?

    A. 16 December 1971 C. 26 January 1972
    B. 23 December 1971 D. 15 August 1972

13. Name of the operation launched by India during the Kargil conflict in 1999?

    A. Operation Blue Star
    B. Operation Gibraltar
    C. Operation Grand Slam
    D. Operation Vijay

14. Which strategic height was captured during the Battle of Tololing in the Kargil war?

    A. Tiger Hill C. Siachen
    B. Tololing D. Drass

15. Which date marked as 'Kargil Vijay Diwas'?

A. 15 August
B. 26 January
C. 26 July
D. 3 December

16. Which summit was held in 1999 to ease diplomatic tension between India and Pakistan?

A. Simla Summit
B. Lahore Summit
C. Agra Summit
D. Delhi Summit

17. Which conflict occurred due to the infiltration of Pakistani paramilitary forces into Indian territory in 1999?

A. 1965 Indo-Pak War
B. 1971 Indo-Pak War
C. Kargil Conflict
D. Siachen Conflict

18. India conducted its nuclear tests in which year?

A. 1995 B. 1996 C. 1997 D. 1998

19. The Pakistani Prime Minister who agreed to withdraw troops during the Kargil conflict was__________.

A. Benazir Bhutto
B. Nawaz Sharif
C. Pervez Musharraf
D. Asif Ali Zardari

20. What was the outcome of the Tashkent Declaration?

A. Permanent peace between India and Pakistan
B. Return to pre-war positions
C. Demilitarization of Kashmir
D. Establishment of the Line of Control

1. C	2. B	3. B	4. C	5. C	6. C	7. A	8. B	9. C	10. B
11. C	12. A	13. D	14. B	15. C	16. B	17. C	18. D	19. B	20. B

06

Introduction to Infantry Weapons and Equipment

6.1 CHARACTERISTICS OF 5.56MM INSAS RIFLE, AMMUNITION, FIREPOWER, STRIPPING, ASSEMBLING AND CLEANING

1. The Word INSAS stands for_________

   A. Indonesian Small Arms System
   B. Indira Small Arms System
   C. Indian Small Arms System
   D. Indigenous Small Arms System

2. INSAS is a _________ of soldier

   A. Personnel Service weapon
   B. Practice weapon
   C. Easy service weapon
   D. Not a service weapon

3. INSAS is manufactured by _________

   A. Defence Research and Development Organization (DRDO)
   B. Defence Research Laboratory (DRL)
   C. Indian Ordinance Factory
   D. Indian Military Academy

4. What is the caliber of 5.56mm INSAS Rifle?

   A. 7.62 mm B. 5.56 mm C. 9 mm D. 6.8 mm

5. What is the length of 5.56mm INSAS Rifle without the bayonet?

   A. 960 mm B. 1110 mm C. 464 mm D. 900 mm

6. What is the effective range of 5.56mm INSAS Rifle?

   A. 200 m B. 300 m C. 400 m D. 500 m

7. What is the weight of the 5.56mm INSAS Rifle with a loaded magazine?

   A. 3.6 kg B. 3.69 kg C. 3.9 kg D. 4.0 kg

8. What is the principle of operation of 5.56mm INSAS Rifle?

   A. Bolt Action
   B. Gas Operated
   C. Recoil Operated
   D. Lever Action

9. What is the normal rate of fire of 5.56mm INSAS Rifle?

   A. 60 rounds/min
   B. 90 rounds/min
   C. 150 rounds/min
   D. 600-650 rounds/min

10. Which mode of fire does 5.56mm INSAS Rifle support?

    A. Fully automatic
    B. Semi-automatic only
    C. Single Shot and Three Round Burst
    D. Burst fire only

11. What type of ammunition is used in the 5.56mm INSAS Rifle?

    A. Ball Round
    B. Tracer Round
    C. Blank Round
    D. All of the above

12. What is the penetration capacity of 5.56mm INSAS Rifle?

    A. 2 mm at 500m
    B. 3 mm at 700m
    C. 4 mm at 600m
    D. 5 mm at 800m

13. What is the weight of 5.56mm INSAS Rifle with full magazine?

    A. 60 gm
    B. 70 gm
    C. 80 gm
    D. 90 gm

14. What is the sight radius of 5.56mm INSAS Rifle?

    A. 450 mm
    B. 460 mm
    C. 470 mm
    D. 480 mm

15. Which part of the 5.56mm INSAS Rifle should not be oiled?

    A. Magazine Catch
    B. Trigger mechanism
    C. Barrel
    D. Rifle spring Assembly

16. What is the intense fire /rapid fire of 5.56mm INSAS Rifle?

    A. 60 rounds/min
    B. 150 rounds/min
    C. 90 rounds/min
    D. 600-650 rounds/min

17. Gas operation of the 5.56mm INSAS Rifle is because of __________

    A. Trigger
    B. Barrel
    C. Piston Extension Assembly
    D. Magazine

18. Which of the following item is used for stripping the extractor of the 5.56mm INSAS Rifle?

    A. Pull through
    B. Drift tool
    C. Chindi
    D. Brush cleaning bore

19. What is the effective range of 5.56mm INSAS Rifle?

    A. 200 m
    B. 300 m
    C. 400 m
    D. 500 m

20. Which item is used to clean the gas cylinder of 5.56mm INSAS Rifle?

    A. Drift tool
    B. Brush cleaning bore
    C. Pull through and chindi
    D. Tool adjusting sight/rear sight

21. What is the cyclic rate of fire of 5.56mm INSAS Rifle?

    A. 60 rounds/min
    B. 90 rounds/min
    C. 150 rounds/min
    D. 600-650 rounds/min

22. Which type of ammunition is NOT used in the INSAS rifle?

    A. Ball Round
    B. Tracer Round
    C. Armor-piercing Round
    D. Blank Round

23. Which part should be checked to ensure the piston extension has completely moved forward after assembling the rifle?

A. Trigger mechanism
B. Change lever
C. Breech box
D. Magazine catch

24. What must be done first to remove the magazine from the 5.56mm INSAS Rifle?

A. Press the trigger
B. Press the magazine catch
C. Cock the rifle
D. Move the change lever to 'R'

1. C	2. A	3. C	4. B	5. A	6. C	7. B	8. B	9. A	10. C
11. D	12. B	13. D	14. C	15. C	16. B	17. C	18. B	19. C	20. C
21. D	22. C	23. B	24. B						

6.2 ORGANISATION OF INFANTRY BATTALION

1. Which is the most important organization in the army?

A. Artillery Battalion
B. Armored Division
C. Infantry Battalion
D. Air Force Wing

2. Which capability allows Infantry Battalion to fight without any outside support?

A. Mobility
B. Self-Reliance
C. Adaptability
D. Vulnerability

3. Which capability allows an infantry battalion to operate effectively in various terrains and climates?

A. Mobility
B. Adaptability
C. Self-Reliance
D. Vulnerability

4. What is the primary role of Infantry Battalion?

   A. To provide medical support
   B. To transport supplies
   C. To hold the ground, move close in with enemy and destroy or capture the enemy
   D. To provide aerial reconnaissance

5. How does the Infantry Battalion overcome its vulnerability in battle?

   A. By relying on air support
   B. By careful sighting, hiding, spreading out, digging, and skilful use of ground
   C. By using heavy artillery
   D. By avoiding combat

6. What are the basic personal weapons used in an infantry battalion?

   A. Pistols, carbines, rifles, and bayonets
   B. Heavy machine guns, rocket launchers, and flamethrowers
   C. Grenade launchers, sniper rifles, and mortars
   D. Anti-tank guided missiles, light machine guns, and automatic grenade launchers

7. What supporting weapons increase the firepower of the Infantry Battalion?

   A. Mortars, machine guns, grenade launchers, and sniper rifles
   B. Artillery cannons, battleships, and bombers
   C. Biological and chemical weapons
   D. Laser and electromagnetic pulse weapons

8. What is the basis of infantry tactics?

   A. Aerial bombardment
   B. Fire and movement
   C. Naval blockade
   D. Cyber warfare

9. What kind of mobility does the Infantry Battalion have?

   A. Limited to road transport
   B. High degree of mobility, capable of overcoming most obstacles
   C. Restricted to urban areas
   D. Only during daytime operations

10. What type of mines are used against infantry?

    A. Naval mines
    B. Anti-tank mines
    C. Anti-personnel mines
    D. Landmines

11. What is the primary role of an infantry battalion?

    A. To provide logistical support
    B. To hold and defend ground
    C. To conduct aerial reconnaissance
    D. To close in with and destroy or capture the enemy

12. What vulnerability does an infantry battalion faces in battle?

    A. Lack of ammunition
    B. Weakness in front of tanks, artillery, small arms, air attack, and anti-personnel mines
    C. Insufficient training
    D. Poor communication

13. What is a key feature of the infantry battalion's organizational capability?

    A. High dependence on external support
    B. Inability to move through obstacles
    C. Limited firepower
    D. High degree of self-reliance and mobility

14. After world war-II, which battle is considered as the largest tank battle in the history?

    A. Battle of Asal Uttar
    B. Battle of Longewala
    C. Battle of Chawinda
    D. Battle of Dograi

15. What was the primary objective of Pakistan's Operation Gibraltar in 1965?

    A. To capture Delhi
    B. To infiltrate forces into Jammu and Kashmir
    C. To destroy Indian Air Force bases
    D. To seize control of Punjab

16. Which weapon is NOT part of the supporting weapons used by an infantry battalion?

    A. Anti-tank guided missiles
    B. Medium machine guns
    C. 81mm mortars
    D. Surface-to-air missiles

17. Which quality is NOT listed as a capability of the infantry battalion?

    A. Self-reliance
    B. Vulnerability
    C. Ability to hold ground
    D. Ability to launch air strikes

1. C	2. B	3. B	4. C	5. B	6. A	7. A	8. B	9. B	10. C
11. D	12. B	13. D	14. C	15. B	16. D	17. D			

6.3 CHARACTERISTICS OF COMPANY SUPPORT WEAPONS

1. What is the caliber of "Dragunov Sniper Rifle"?

   A. 5.56 mm
   B. 7.62 mm
   C. 9 mm
   D. 12.7 mm

2. What is the effective range of "Dragunov Sniper Rifle" with a telescope sight?

   A. 800 meters
   B. 1000 meters
   C. 1300 meters
   D. 1500 meters

3. What is the magazine capacity of "Dragunov Sniper Rifle"?

   A. 5 rounds
   B. 10 rounds
   C. 15 rounds
   D. 20 rounds

4. What type of ammunition is NOT used in the "Dragunov Sniper Rifle"?

   A. Armor Piercing
   B. Tracer
   C. Hollow Point
   D. Incendiary

5. What is the weight of "7.62 mm Medium Machine Gun" (MMG) without the tripod?

   A. 10.2 kg B. 12.5 kg C. 14.2 kg D. 16.0 kg

6. How many rounds are there in the belt of "7.62 mm Medium Machine Gun?

   A. 100 rounds C. 200 rounds
   B. 150 rounds D. 235 rounds

7. What is the cyclic rate of fire of "7.62 mm Medium Machine Gun" is?

   A. 100-200 rounds per minute
   B. 200-300 rounds per minute
   C. 350-400 rounds per minute
   D. 500-1000 rounds per minute

8. What is the beaten zone of "7.62 mm Medium Machine Gun" at a range of 600 meters?

   A. 100m x 1m C. 50m x 4m
   B. 65m x 3m D. 110m x 1m

9. What is the weight of "30 mm Automatic Grenade Launcher" (AGL) without the sight?

   A. 12 kg B. 14.5 kg C. 18 kg D. 20 kg

10. What is the normal rate of fire of "30 mm Automatic Grenade Launcher"?

    A. 50 grenades per minute
    B. 150 grenades per minute
    C. 100 grenades per minute
    D. 200 grenades per minute

11. What is the maximum range for the HE round of "84 mm Rocket Launcher" (RL)?

    A. 400 meters
    B. 500 meters
    C. 1000 meters
    D. 1300 meters

12. What type of ammunition is NOT used in the "84 mm Rocket Launcher"?

    A. HEAT
    B. HE
    C. Smoke
    D. Tracer

13. What is the back-blast area of "84 mm Rocket Launcher"?

    A. 10 meters
    B. 15 meters
    C. 20 meters
    D. 25 meters

14. What is the rate of fire of "84 mm Rocket Launcher"?

    A. 3 rounds per minute
    B. 6 rounds per minute
    C. 9 rounds per minute
    D. 12 rounds per minute

15. What is the diameter of the area illuminated by the Illumination round of the "84 mm Rocket Launcher"?

    A. 300-400 meters
    B. 400-500 meters
    C. 500-600 meters
    D. 600-700 meters

16. 7.62 mm Dragunov Sniper Rifle, 7.62mm Medium Machine Gun(MMG), 30 mm Automatic Grenade Launcher(AGL) and 84 mm Rocket Launcher(RL), all these weapons are ________

    A. Infantry service weapons
    B. Infantry regular practice weapons
    C. Infantry Support weapons
    D. Infantry made weapons

1. B	2. C	3. B	4. C	5. C	6. D	7. D	8. A	9. C	10. A
11. C	12. D	13. B	14. B	15. B	16. C				

6.4 CHARACTERISTICS OF INFANTRY BATTALION SUPPORT WEAPONS

1. What is the caliber of the "81mm Mortar"?

   A. 75 mm B. 81 mm C. 90 mm D. 100 mm

2. What is the weight of "81mm Mortar" without the sight?

   A. 30.5 kg B. 35.6 kg C. 40.6 kg D. 45.6 kg

3. What is the maximum range of "81mm Mortar"?

   A. 4500 m B. 4800 m C. 5000 m D. 5200 m

4. What is the slow rate of fire of "81mm Mortar"?

   A. 3-5 rounds per minute
   B. 6-8 rounds per minute
   C. 12-14 rounds per minute
   D. 9-11 rounds per minute

5. What is the maximum muzzle velocity of "81mm Mortar"?

   A. 200 m/sec C. 305 m/sec
   B. 250 m/sec D. 350 m/sec

6. What is the elevation limit of "81mm Mortar"?

   A. 30 to 70 degrees C. 40 to 80 degrees
   B. 35 to 75 degrees D. 45 to 85 degrees

7. What is the minimum range of "Anti-Tank Guided Missile" (ATGM)?

   A. 50 m B. 75 m C. 100 m D. 125 m

8. What is the maximum range of "Anti-Tank Guided Missile" (ATGM)?

   A. 2000 m B. 2250 m C. 2500 m D. 2750 m

9. What is the rate of fire of "Anti-Tank Guided Missile" (ATGM)?

   A. 1 missile per minute C. 2 missiles per minute
   B. 4 missiles per minute D. 3 missiles per minute

10. What is the hit probability of "Anti-Tank Guided Missile" (ATGM)?

    A. 70% to 80% C. 85% to 90%
    B. 80% to 85% D. 90% to 96%

11. What is the accuracy of "Anti-Tank Guided Missile" (ATGM) at maximum range?

    A. 40 cm around the point of aim
    B. 60 cm around the point of aim
    C. 50 cm around the point of aim
    D. 70 cm around the point of aim

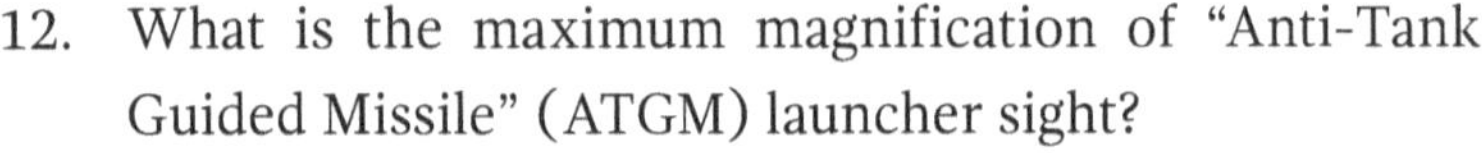

12. What is the maximum magnification of "Anti-Tank Guided Missile" (ATGM) launcher sight?

    A. 8 times
    B. 10 times
    C. 12 times
    D. 14 times

13. What type of guidance system is used by the "Anti-Tank Guided Missile" (ATGM)?

    A. Laser guided
    B. Radar guided
    C. Wire guided
    D. GPS guided

14. What is the penetration power of "Anti-Tank Guided Missile" (ATGM) at a 90-degree angle of impact?

    A. 300 mm B. 400 mm C. 460 mm D. 500 mm

15. What is the safety distance for flanking the "81mm Mortar"?

    A. 150 m B. 200 m C. 250 m D. 300 m

1. B	2. C	3. D	4. B	5. C	6. D	7. B	8. C	9. D
10. D	11. B	12. B	13. C	14. C	15. B			

www.ingramcontent.com/pod-product-compliance
Lightning Source LLC
LaVergne TN
LVHW041139150826
845673LV00001B/49

9798896106760